JOURNEY TO EMOTIONAL HEALTH

FROM BROKENNESS TO WHOLENESS

SAMUKILE R. TAKAVINGOFA

Wholeness
Incorporated
Publishing

Journey to Emotional Health

First Published in 2020
E-mail: samutakavingofa@gmail.com
Tel: +1 202 820 7801

Cover Design by: **Milton Mudzengerere**
Typesetting, Graphics and Layout: **Marshal Chiza**

ISBN: 9798558143706

DEDICATION

To every individual who seeks to live a full life which God purposefully ordained for them in spite of the challenges and adversities of this life.

CONTENTS

ACKNOWLEDGEMENTS

I am grateful to God my Maker, the One who knew and installed purpose in me before my conception. Him who ordered and still orders my footsteps to date, with Him nothing just happens, because He is sovereign in every season of our lives. To Him be all glory, honor and praise for allowing me to have gone through everything I went through so that His will may be done in and through me. I thank my Lord and Savior Jesus Christ for saving me and allowing me to journey to a place of wholeness and gave me the grace to minister this wholeness to others.

To my loving husband Bob, for allowing me to be the woman God created me to be, and never allowing me to settle for mediocre, always encouraging me to be and do the best. I appreciate your love and support throughout this project and the many crazy ideas I come up with. Thank you for being a friend in the journey and standing by me through all seasons- loving you always...

My beloved children in whom I am well pleased, Thandeka, Mandipaishe and Anashe - my little miracles, always reminding me of how faithful God is. When I look at you and listen to you, I know I am experiencing God's love in the flesh, you are for signs and wonders. I appreciate how you love me and celebrate me always. You genuinely believe I am a superwoman! How cool is that?

My Dad Bishop Freddy Thokozani Ngadziore, you have taught me faith, you showed me genuine love, you have celebrated me, you have always believed in me. In the face of doubt and fear the motto you gave us from when we were little that "A Ngadziore never fails" has kept me going.

My Mum Pheobe Ngadziore, My prayer warrior. Thank you for being that pillar of strength for me, always encouraging me and reminding me of how valuable I am. Your big heart and love has been a powerful foundation that has taught me what I have is not only for me but for the benefit of humanity. You have shown me that love never fails – I love you, I love you, I love you *mhamha* -in your voice.

My biggest fans - my siblings, Sethukile Mpopoma my womb mate, God knew I would need that one constant friend who will always be there, I love you *mwana wamudhara*, Sis Rachael Chidembo thank you for being a great example. My one and only brother, the great leader, Ronald Ngadziore I appreciate who you are. My baby sis Nyasha Madyara, a friend of friends I know I will never walk alone. Maiguru Nishia my sister in love, you are loved and appreciated so much.

My Mentors Mrs Doreen Mukwena, Mrs Eunice Njovana, Pastor Cynthia Chirinda, Pastor Rumbidzayi Kamba thank you for believing in me and in the vision. I am indebted to your unwavering support, teaching and encouragement in becoming the woman I am today.

I appreciate my spiritual father, Apostle and Prophet Andrew Wutawunashe for laboring in me and tirelessly sharing the word of life that has helped me know God for myself.

To sis Mildred Gloria Muchena and 'Boo' Kudzai Helene-Rose Rufuse for doing the first book edits before Wholeness Incorporated finalized the whole project, may the Lord reward you for your selflessness diligence and excellence, I appreciate you

To all those I have coached, counselled and ministered to on my journey, you have helped me grow in wisdom, knowledge and understanding.

I would like to express my gratitude to every man and woman who has encouraged me and motivated me to pursue my calling and purpose. All my friends who have encouraged me and spoken words of wisdom and prophecy over my life, and those who contributed to the book in ways that perhaps they don't even realize. Mentioning you all would fill pages, but you know who you are, I appreciate and love you all.

FOREWORD

"...I urgently need to come and see you because I feel it's time for me to now align with what God is calling me to do in this season..."

I vividly remember this conversation with Samu one morning some years ago, as she boldly stepped out and connected with me to pre-empt what has now become a life transforming vision across the world. The conversations and events that followed thereafter bore testimony that indeed the season had come for the deep ministry for inner healing in Samu to be unleashed to the world. I cannot remember a single event I attended where the overwhelming presence of God was not released to deliver souls that had been trapped in captivity for so long. In spite of its humble beginnings, Tamar Restoration Centre consistently touched lives and communities in Zimbabwe and beyond from the very onset. The vision and the visionary are a true testimony of walking by faith and not by sight.

To know Samu is to know a God yielded vessel who walks in absolute authenticity and humility. Her unique skills for listening have led so many people to a place of unburdening their souls in a way they had never thought possible. This book, *The Journey to Emotional Health* is a toolbox and manual for any individual who suspects that the life they are living has been hijacked by emotional dysfunction. In her first chapter, Journey Back to Me, is a special outpouring of grace to enable every individual to locate themselves on the campus of their God ordained path. The ensuing chapters on Self-Love, Dealing with Rejection and Forgiveness are foundational pillars that Samu has provided for the reader to detoxify themselves as they set off on their journey to emotional health.

Synonymous with any journey, is the need to pause, rest and reflect. Whilst this book is very difficult to put down, I highly recommend that the reader takes time to introspect, review their life and commit to actions that will see them to their destined and God ordained greatness. I have been so blessed to be one of the first readers to receive the inner healing ministry that flows from every single page in this book. All of us have areas that need realignment and redirection with our prophetic destiny. I pray that as you read through the wisdom and virtue that flows from this book, you would indeed have a divine encounter with your wholeness.

In the same way that Samu called me on that morning with a sense of urgency to unleash this powerful ministry of wholeness, I believe that it is God's will for you to enter into emotional liberty without delay. Every year that you have lost to emotional dysfunction must be restored to you with urgency so that you can live a fulfilled life of impact on this earth. I urge you to take seriously

every prayer, reflection and exercise that she has
shared with you in this book.

May wholeness be your portion in every area of
your life!

Cynthia Chirinda
Author, Strategist, Life Coach.
Founder and Managing Consultant – Wholeness Incorporated

INTRODUCTION

I vividly remember sitting alone, sad, depressed and wondering how I got to this point. I felt so hopeless and overwhelmed and unable to change my situation. I went back and forth in my mind remembering what I recalled as the happiest times of my childhood and the glory "uni" days. I wondered if I would ever see the door of happiness again in my life. I felt like I had been sentenced to a life of sadness, and I just needed to suck it up. I knew that ending my life was not an option so what was left for me was to accept what was meant to be. I couldn't help thinking that perhaps I was one of those destined for misfortune. I felt as if I would be one of those who had to fight for everything in my life and that a simple thing like holding a child in my arms would have to come after sacrificing another. As if that was not enough, I was just generally unhappy and I blamed people around me for not doing enough to make me happy. I felt like such a failure and as if there was nothing I could do right, and that there was enough evidence to prove that. Feeling this low also resulted in the abandonment of the dreams I had nurtured as a young girl. In fact, I couldn't remember those dreams anyway and I just went through each day like a zombie, watching my days just wasting away while pain took center stage in my life.

Conquering these emotions was a miraculous process which began with the realization of God's unconditional love for me and His mission to make me happy through giving me abundant life. The process began before I even realized I was being processed for better. It was only later on in the process that I could define milestones in my growth. I was surprised that I could actually be happy with myself for no apparent reason. What amazed me the most is that not much had changed around me - battles and challenges were still a big part of my experience. It was my attitude and perception of these experiences that had changed. That is when I realized that I had been, and was going through a journey to Emotional Health. I knew in my heart I could not keep calm, I had to share this new-found journey with others who had been through what I had been through. I actually realized that what I thought was the end of the world, was nothing compared to the turbulence others were facing in their own lives. All I knew was that there is hope for all of us, no matter how rough we think we have had it in life.

Step by step, I could define the significant milestones that led me to this place of wholeness, and I needed to share these with others who have felt this sense of helplessness I had felt before. I could tell I had been through a journey, from a place of brokenness to wholeness. As I began to record these milestones and share them with others, I realized that God had transformed my pain into purpose. My process from pain to wholeness had become a manual for someone else out there and I could clearly define it as *"The Journey to Emotional Health"*

So now I share this journey to Emotional Health with the hope that other people can get to their place of wholeness. Having gone through the season I describe above helped me realize that being emotionally unhealthy carries the ability to derail God's plans and purpose over one's life. When I began to gain more clarity on this journey, it took me back to 2004, when I was studying at the University of Cape Town in South Africa. At that time, I was living in an apartment with a close friend of mine and remember how we affectionately called that place "The Mead" because of the most joy filled memories we shared in that place. We often joyfully laugh about those days as friends would join us for fun times in "The Mead". This is one season I would not mind going back to in life as we had very few cares back then. It was at that place - No 102 Queensmead, where God visited me concerning my purpose. I was sitting in my room listening to a cassette on my small stereo (that's revealing my age there). A lady was preaching about Tamar, king David's daughter who was raped by her own brother Amnon. What struck me as I listened to her reading that account was that the last thing we heard about Tamar is that she lay desolate in her brother's house. 2 Samuel 13: 20 *"And Absalom her brother said to her. "Has Amnon your brother been with you? But now hold your peace, my sister. He is your brother, do not take this thing to heart.* **"So Tamar remained desolate in her brother Absalom's** *house"*

In this experience God made me realize that going through intense life challenges and traumas can significantly alter one's life, bringing them to places of utter desolation. The Oxford Dictionary defines desolation as a state of complete emptiness or devastation, solitary misery, wretchedness and hopelessness. Quite like the state I described as I began this chapter. Desolation can kill the will in you to live, let alone pursue your dreams. As I carefully considered Tamar's story during my extraordinary moment with God that day, I knew in my inner knower that my purpose was to lift people up from that place of desolation. The things around fulfilling my purpose however, came together many years later - after I went through my own season of desolation.

The birthing of the Journey to Emotional Health is a powerful tool to help people out of their place of desolation so that they are able to live out their God given purpose and be who God has called them to be. It is Bible based tool that provides you with life-skills to navigate through the wounded spaces of your soul all the way to wholeness. It also equips you with resilience to navigate curveballs that may come your way through life's challenging experiences. It is a personal and non-prescriptive tool which acknowledges the uniqueness of everyone's story.

Every one's journey is different as our experiences are all unique. The levels to which we perceive and handle our emotional wounds and places of brokenness is different. The key to this journey is that no matter where one finds themselves, they need to begin their journey because wholeness is your portion.

CHAPTER 1

JOURNEY BACK TO ME

Authentic Identity -Who Am I?

O Lord, thou hast searched me, and known me. Thou knowest my downsitting and mine uprising, thou understandest my thought afar off." - Psalms 139:1-2 KJV

More than 15 years ago, I received my life's purpose and vision to open Tamar Restoration Centre (TRC). I understood that it was to operate as a nonprofit organization (NGO) committed to giving women resources for wholeness. During this time, I was a very ambitious, tenacious and unstoppable young woman. I had such bold and radical faith, such that even in the difficult economic climate in Zimbabwe, I applied to go and study at a university in South Africa which my parents could not even afford. God honored my faith and made a way for me to be enrolled at the South African university against all odds. As a student, I continued to trust in God for provision until I miraculously landed a job on campus.

When I completed my studies, I returned to Zimbabwe and thought my life was on course and headed for success when I found a good job with an NGO. But as life always has it, curves and bumps began to come my way, with experiences that threw me off course and off balance. Soon after a glorious wedding, I lost my job, had miscarriages and faced challenges from many directions. Although from a distance my marriage looked intact the challenges my husband and I faced shook our union. With all these events taking place, I never realized during this difficult process that I was slowly losing something invaluable.

My big epiphany happened years later during a discussion with a close friend after one of the prayer meetings we used to have with a group of ladies. As my friend was explaining to me a series of events in her life she said, **"Samu do you know I came to a point where I forgot who I was"**. It was in that very moment that it also dawned on me that I was also at a point in my life where I did not remember who I was anymore. It was as if a light bulb had been switched on inside my soul and all of a sudden, I could see this hole that was in my life. I realized that the Samu I knew many years back, the dreamer, the tenacious and radical one had vanished. I could not relate to the person who I had become, to the point where I could no longer answer simple questions like, 'what is it that I enjoy doing?'. This reality hit me hard, **"I did not know who I was anymore"**.

I left the prayer meeting with a myriad of thoughts, questions and emotions flooding my whole being. I could not comprehend how it all happened, how it is that I had forgotten who I was. As I battled in my new-found revelation, I realized that the one thing the devil fights so much is you knowing who you are and discovering your authentic identity. Most of the challenges the devil brings your way are targeted at making you slowly forget who you truly are. He knows that the moment you know who you are, you become a threat to his kingdom because you start operating in the knowledge of your full identity. When you are operating from a place of not knowing who you really are, you are harmless to him.

For instance, a world changer who thinks they are a loser will not make any difference in the world until they start living in their true identity of being a world changer. One of the greatest crises in the kingdom of God is an identity crisis. This is not knowing or being unsure of who you really are - your 'Authentic Identity'. This usually happens when the enemy brings a series of challenges your way such as pain, rejection, tragedy or failure. Through these challenges people tend to identify themselves according to their trouble and forget who God said they are as well as whose they are.

It is critical that at every point in life, despite the challenges you face that you continue to hold on to your true identity. Always asking yourself "who am I?' Discovering your authentic identity is critical for one to live a full life as well as living out your purpose. This is because when you know who you are, your outer circumstances don't intimate your inner conviction. To take this even a step further, when you know who you are, you are fit for the Masters' use. As you discover who you are, your purpose in life starts manifesting and you can confidently live it out because it defines you.

The Impact of Negative Experiences On Authentic Identity

The devil is always lurking in the prefix of the negative experiences we go through to gradually take us to the place where we forget who we are. These negative life experiences and challenges have the capacity to wound one's soul leaving them in a state of confusion as to who they really are. Others may have never had an opportunity to discover their authentic identity from birth. This could be due to life's experiences they were birthed into which may have sadly become a toxic environment characterized by elements such as rejection, abuse or extreme poverty. For some, it could have been challenges and painful experiences that showed up later in life. These experiences can potentially cause scars that one eventually carries from childhood through events like abuse, rejection, bullying at school or failure to fit in peer groups. Other times it can be a result of someone significant in one's life continuously saying negative things about them such that you end up receiving and believing those negative words about yourself.

I remember a friend sharing with me that her husband used to refer to her as *"Pfende"*; a word that means "dirty/untidy." Her husband continuously addressed her with this degrading term and would do all he can to justify his continuous rhetoric by finding specks of dust in the most unlikely places. My friend slowly began to lose confidence in who she was and her abilities. She started believing and taking on this identity assigned to her by her husband. As time progressed, she internalized this and ultimately believed that she was such an untidy woman who could not keep her house clean to save her life. This experience among other negativities literally paralyzed her self-esteem and distorted her understanding of who she was.

Another lady shared with me how she ended up finding herself on a resuscitation bed in hospital due to the impact of the emotional abuse and words she received from her spouse. Unchecked loss of authentic identity can reach an extreme breaking point or even slowly send you to the grave. This is one reason I am passionate about addressing these issues because their negative impact can be devastating.

Your Response to Negative Experiences Matter

The best response to such cases where your identity is stripped away from you through negative words that come from others, is to remember that no one can make you inferior without your consent. You cannot control what people say and think about you, the only thing you can control is your response. One of the biggest mistakes people make is that they accept these negative words and begin to believe them. When you begin to understand and know better, you develop the capacity to refuse negative words spoken to you and begin telling yourself that you are who God says you are.

This reminds me of a Zimbabwean talk show host - Mrs Rebecca Chisamba. During her "Mai Chisamba Shows", when someone is making a contribution she feels is off topic or she does not agree with she responds in a way I find very interesting. She says, *"mafungire avo varovereyi maoko!"* (*"Those are his/her thoughts give them a round of applause!"*) In such moments she will not waste her energy arguing even though she may not agree with the participant's view. This was a very important lesson as it taught me to not engage with negative words spoken to me. I used to repeat this phrase both verbally and sometimes in my heart. You need to refuse the negative words said about you without losing any energy by trying to prove otherwise. Be aware of this, anything contrary to what God says about you is not you. This means it is YOUR responsibility to protect your identity.

The Bible says that you shall know the truth and the truth shall set you free. It is the truth that you know that will set you free. Knowing who you are in Christ, your authentic identity will set you free.

Some people have for so many years been imprisoned by bad words someone spoke into their life. It does not matter who they are, do not allow yourself to be imprisoned because you have power to set yourself free. The battle begins in your mind, that is why the Bible says "....*For out of the abundance of the heart the mouth speaks*" Matthew 12:24. If in your mind you have received negative words, you will find yourself unconsciously speaking that way about yourself. Always remember that life and death is in the power of your tongue, you are therefore able to awaken your authentic identity through the words of your mouth.

Overcome 'Self-Hate' With The Positive Affirmations- The 'I Am"

Unfortunately, there are times when you are your own worst enemy, where it is not others speaking negatively to you, but you, saying all sorts of negative things about yourself and being your worst critique. Harboring negative thoughts about yourself and becoming your worst critique is very harmful. It is a mockery to God who made you because you are His masterpiece. This attitude insults what He has done for and in you. Make it your responsibility to be the first person to speak positive words over your life through God's Word and remember - it is your responsibility!
I have decided each morning to declare my "I AM's" - my identity, that is, who I am in Christ. I tell myself everyday as I look in the mirror. This is a powerful and life changing exercise which I

encourage you to do if you have not been doing it. You need to remove the negatives in your mind by filling it with the positives.

Below are examples of some 'I AM' statements that I had to start declaring on my journey to finding my true identity based on what God has said about me:

I am beautiful,
I am made in the image God
I am fearfully and wonderfully made
I am blessed
I am favored
I am Hephzibah, God delights in me
I am loved
I am accepted in the beloved
I am unique
I am protected
I am forgiven
I am redeemed
I am a winner
I am the head and not the tail
I am above only and not beneath
I am outstanding
I am anointed
I am a history maker
I am influential
I am powerful
I am well able
I am confident
I can do all things ...

The list goes on.

This is who you are in Christ so declare it until your mind knows and believes it. Instead of spending time meditating on the negative words that have pained you, erase those negative words and replace them with your 'I am' statements.

In taking my journey back to my authentic Identity, the 'I am' exercise really brought great transformation in me. I noticed that some things in my life began to happen in a miraculous way simply because of the power of the tongue. Mark 11:23 says this *"For verily I say unto you, that whosoever shall say unto this mountain, Be thou removed, and be thou cast into the sea; and shall not doubt in his heart, but shall believe that those things which he saith shall come to pass; he shall have whatsoever he saith"*. This scripture reveals that words have power. God, Himself created the heavens and the earth by the Word of His mouth. This is the same power and authority God gave us through the word of our mouths. If you understood how you can literally move mountains through the spoken word, you would be able to transform your life by declaring who God says you are.

The work of discovering authentic identity must begin in the mind. You need to be renewed in the way your mind thinks. You begin this journey by first remembering that you are made in God's image. This means that what is true about you is only what God said about you. Even in the moments where your thoughts are not in line with the Word of God, let God be true and every man a liar. Embrace only the truth from God's Word and make it your reality.

Know Your Wounds

In pursuit of your authentic Identity another important aspect to consider for introspection is knowing your wounds. As I shared my story in the earlier parts of this chapter, I related how I came to the realization that I no longer recognized who I was. This had come about due to a lot of pressures, challenges and negative things that had happened to me in the course of time. As you start boldly journeying back to who you truly are, it is also important to take deeper introspection of your life by understanding your journey and what it is that stripped your identity away. Often times it is wounds in our soul that break us and eventually bring about self-doubt preventing us from discovering our Authentic Identity.

In your journey to self-discovery it is important that you get to know your wounds. Wounds which strip you of your identity. These wounds can come from relationship challenges, tragic events or issues of life that weigh us down. Knowing your wounds enables you to face and get them healed. Unhealed wounds impact our future negatively and tend to distort authentic Identity.

There was a point in my life where I experienced so much rejection to an extent that made me so desperate for approval and acceptance but did not receive it. This wounded me so badly even though

I did not realize it. I projected extreme insecurity. When I discovered these wounds and became conscious that I needed healing, I began to make precise declarations which were therapy to the wounds I carried. I was very precise, saying things like, "I am accepted in the beloved, I am loved, I am approved by God". Slowly I began to receive my healing and began operating with confidence. I became more secure in myself because I knew I was accepted and approved by God. My desperate need for peoples' approval began to fade away.

Wounded people have a tendency of projecting their pain onto others unawares. Investigating any wounds you may have, will help you to become precise in your search for healing so that you will project to others who God says you are. The most powerful stage is discovering and acknowledging that you have wounds and allowing the healing process to begin. This is a process through which you become aware of the effect your wounds have on others empowering you to become more conscious of your actions and reactions. You begin to parent yourself, trusting God for healing and reaching out for that real identity you have in Christ not the identity being projected by your wounds.

Get Rid Of Condemnation

Condemnation is another powerful tool the devil uses to distort your identity, Romans 8: 1 says *"Therefore, there is no more condemnation to those that are in Christ Jesus"*. It is important that we learn to forgive ourselves because the devil is always waiting to remind us of our mistakes and bring condemnation to us. Whenever the devil brings condemnation to your face, you need to respond by telling him that you are redeemed, washed in the blood, and hence you are forgiven meaning there is no more condemnation. You need to realize and accept that you are not perfect and that you make mistakes. These errors that we make should not define us and by no means become our identity, simply because we are human. Embrace the love and grace of Jesus Christ. If Christ forgave you, you have no right not to forgive yourself. Please forgive yourself, receive the truth of who God says you are, because that is who you truly are.

Answering The 'Who Am I?' Question

The journey to Emotional Health, is a process that can take you out of your comfort zone, because you are challenging things that have seemed normal for a long time. I have noted in the groups I have worked with, that people struggle to answer the "Who am I" question. Below I try to give clarity on aspects people commonly confuse their identity with and explain what is and what is not your authentic identity.

1. Marital status
Being someone's wife or husband is not who you are because it is a God given role which does not

define the authentic you. God forbid, in the event that your spouse leaves you or passes on, the authentic you, continues to live on even when such events happen. The mistake some people make- especially women, is having this sense of accomplishment because one is married and now uses prefix 'Mrs.' Other women make the mistake of feeling a sense of being inadequate simply because they are not someone's wife yet. Your identity is more than this God given role.

2. Being a parent

Being a parent is not your authentic identity. It is a biological role of procreation which comes with a responsibility of taking care of your offspring. You can fulfill this role but it does not necessarily define who you truly are.

3. Your Job

Defining yourself based on your profession does not define your authentic identity because your job is your occupation and not who you are. In the event that you retire or lose your job the authentic you continues to live on. Be aware that when God deals with us He doesn't deal with us in reference to our roles be it marital or occupational, He calls us by our names. Sarah in the Bible who had been named Sarai before had her name changed and given to her by God. The name Sara which God gave her defined her purpose to be the mother of many nations. Abraham previously known as Abram had his name changed by God linked to his calling also. One significant lesson we learn from Sarah was that she fought to defend her purpose, resulting in her having to send away Hagar even though Hagar was her mistake. God deals with us as individuals and expects us to deliver when it comes to our purpose.

Although we have roles and responsibilities which we will be accountable to God for, the core of our existence is purpose. When you know who you are and begin to operate in line with that calling, you will experience a sense of fulfillment and joy that you cannot explain. This is why the question, 'who am I?' should always be at the back of your mind. It is the force that drives your existence. Finding yourself is something that is intrinsic. Jeremiah 1: 5 says *"Before I formed thee in the belly I knew thee; and before thou camest forth out of the womb I sanctified thee, and I ordained thee a prophet unto the nations"*. When God formed you in the womb, he placed an assignment and purpose over your life. This assignment is what we define as authentic identity, who you really are. When you are able to discover and answer to this assignment you are living in your authentic identity. As you go through this journey allow God to reveal to you who you are. When you know who you are, you start living in the capacity of God's assignment on your life. There is no-one who comes into this world without a purpose. The moment you are created, an assignment is already attached to your name.

Discovery of purpose is another important topic we will revisit later in this book. Purpose answers the needs of others. Your area of purpose is often one which you feel passionate about and tend to gravitate towards. It may also be an issue that you have a burden about or one that really worries you. You need to make a relentless effort to discover what your purpose is, because therein lies your Authentic Identity.

Knowing Christ-Salvation

Knowing who you are means nothing when it is not based on a solid foundation of knowing whose you are. As you pursue your authentic identity, it is important for you to know that being a child of God is the most important Identity you can have as you go through life. Your Identity and how you define yourself is the most powerful source that will propel you to your greatness. The devil will fight tooth and nail to confuse you in this regard. He will bring experiences and negative words from people that will make you doubt who you are. If your identity is not anchored in Christ, it will continue to shift with every situation that you face in life.

God made us in His image and His quest is to always reconcile us back to Him so that we are called by His name. God will never see us any different, even in our own dysfunction He will still love us. Knowing your identity as a child of God will put you in a place of advantage no matter what you face. He is always drawing us closer to Him through His unconditional love. This means that situations will come and go, people will hurt you, people will reject you, bad things will happen. But when your Identity is anchored in Christ you will always be victorious. Knowing that you are a child of God will give you authority over situations. You begin to realize that you are seated with Christ in the heavens and that you have authority over evil. Hurts will come but you will overcome when sitting with Christ.

Ephesians 2:6-7 tells us that, *"And hath raised us up together and made us sit together in heavenly places in Christ Jesus: That in the ages to come he might shew the exceeding riches of his grace in his kindness toward us through Christ Jesus."*

You will be strengthened, healed and made whole in Him. One song I love to sing that reminds me of this is by Jonathan & Melissa Helser, which says:

> *"I am no longer a slave to fear,*
> *I am a Child of God"*.

I want to encourage everyone reading this to ensure that your identity is anchored in Him. If you have not made Jesus Christ the Lord and Savior of your life, I encourage you to give your life to Him today so that He deals with all your issues. Some might have been confused by all the bad things that have happened in your life but know that He still loves you so much.

In the section below I have written a prayer for you to ask Jesus into your life if you haven't done so or if you feel that you have strayed away from Him over time. The journey to wholeness cannot be complete if you don't have Jesus as the anchor. Take some time to pray this prayer below if you need to receive Jesus Christ as your personal Lord and Saviour.

Prayer:
'Dear Lord Jesus, thank you for loving me. I acknowledge that I might have strayed away from your love. I come to you today, asking you to be Lord of my life. Thank you for saving me and making me a CHILD OF GOD. I am yours from today. In Jesus name, Amen'

If you have prayed this prayer with all your heart, Jesus has come into your heart. Begin to pursue a relationship with God, and ask God to reveal Himself to you. The greatest gift you can give yourself is having clarity on who you are and whose you are. So that no matter what you face, you know that "You are a Child of God"

CHAPTER 2

SELF-LOVE

Another critical pillar which totally transformed my life from the inside out, is learning to love myself. Loving oneself is one of the most important things a person can do in order to achieve a satisfying, meaningful and joy-filled life. The Bible text in Mark 12:31 puts it this way, *"And the second is like, namely this; Thou shalt love thy neighbor as <u>thyself</u>. There is none other commandment greater than these"*.

This text here indicates that you can only love others to the extent that you love yourself. If you do not love yourself, your love for others will be very limited because you will be trying to give from an empty cup. Be aware of this, loving yourself is the foundation of flourishing Emotional Health. If you harbor and nurse negative thoughts and emotions about yourself, you are setting yourself up for so much depression and sadness in life. Our number one emotional need is love, and you should be the first to give yourself love before you expect it from others. The world out there is very unkind, people you trust will betray you, people will say what they think about you, people can crush you and break your heart, that's just how life can be. Why don't you be the first person to love yourself and teach people how to treat you?

The big question I have for you is this, "is it possible that you are the greatest enemy to yourself and your progress in life?" Most people don't realize how lack of self-love is pulling them backwards and could possibly be the major reason they are so unhappy in their lives. Some people are their own worst critic and have no kind words to speak about themselves.

I recall a time in my life where everything seemed to be on the downward trail. I was so sad and depressed. Little did I realize that my sadness and depression were projecting on the people around me. Though in my mind I was working hard to do acts of love to others, I later realized that I had neglected loving and taking care of myself. Be aware that self-love and self-care are not acts of selfishness but rather "self-fulness." Self- fulness is the choice to become the best version of yourself so that you are able to give what is in you to others.

The funny thing is that when we lose ourselves while trying to build our families and others around us, we tend to give less and less to these people we are losing ourselves to. You can't give the best of you when you do not know how to love yourself. God wishes for us to be whole, for our souls to prosper. A soul that is deprived of love cannot thrive. It is only a matter of time before that deprived soul slowly diminishes and shrivels due to lack of love.

On the Maslow hierarchy of needs, love is one of the basic needs that human beings need to survive. Love is the life blood of relationships and knowing that you are loved gives a sense of belonging and helps you to go on. A loveless life is a miserable life and that is the reason you find that Christ's greatest commandment for us is to love one another. He also explained that you can only love others to the extent you love yourself, meaning you cannot give that which you have not given to yourself. It hurts me to see people who commit suicide, or young ladies who are so desperate to be loved they are willing to lose everything they stand for to the extent that they give away their dignity and their bodies and are left with no self-respect.

Where It All Begins

In learning to understand what love is and how you can learn to love yourself and others, it is important that you know the source of love and where to draw that love from. John 4:7-8 puts it this way *"⁷ Beloved, let us love one another: for love is of God; and everyone that loveth is born of God, and* knoweth God.[8] *He that loveth not knoweth not God; for God is love.*" Realizing that the ultimate source and example of what love is, begins with knowing God, because God is the love that we are all seeking for.

In order to be able to experience real unconditional Love, you need to get plugged in to Gods unfailing love for you. The ultimate example of what love is, is God the father Himself, who demonstrated His love to us, that while we were sinners Christ died for us. Not when we were already perfect, but in our imperfection, He demonstrated His love. God loves us so much and already paid the ultimate price of allowing His son Jesus to die for us all. All you need to do is to receive His love so that you can experience what love is, and thereafter become a conduit of that love to yourself and then others.

Knowing, embracing and understanding God's love is the key that will help us to love ourselves. *"That Christ may dwell in your hearts by faith, that ye may be rooted and grounded in love, May be able to comprehend with all saints what is the breadth, and the length, and depth, and height; And to know the love of Christ, which passeth all knowledge, that ye might be filled with all the fullness of God."* Ephesians 3:17-20

Coming to the full realization that God loves you unconditionally and has accepted you into the beloved should thresh away any feelings of rejection by other people. When some people experience rejection from man, they get confused and begin to think that they are unloved, they do not realize that men's love can fall short because of human imperfection. The key is to know that God's love is the perfect love and that is what everyone needs to be connected to in order to be able to experience the full expression of perfect love.

God's love for you is so great such that even if you were the only one on this planet, Jesus would have come to die for you. Whenever doubt tries to seep into your mind remember this, you are loved. It doesn't matter who you were expecting to have loved you, but then rejected you. It could be a mother, father, lover or whoever it could be, know that you are loved. What is important is that you receive the love of Christ in your heart of hearts. Let this love bind your broken heart and remove all doubt and negativity. Even when you mess up, God's unconditional love is waiting to embrace you. Tell yourself every day that you are loved and let the love of God permeate every part of your being.

Meditating on the practical description of what love entails, according to 1st Corinthians 13, is one way through which you can understand the meaning of true love. When you can take these attributes like, love is kind, love does not keep record of wrongs, love does not rejoice in the evil but rejoices in the good, love does not fail. You then begin to apply these attributes of love to yourself in their totality. This will enable you to love yourself to God's standard.

The more time you spend with someone, the more you get to understand them and the more you get closer to the other person. That is the experience you get when you start loving you and getting closer to you. It is an amazing feeling because the best relationship you can have with anyone apart from God is the relationship you have with yourself. Self-love is the best gift you can give yourself.

Another dimension to this is that when you love yourself you are honoring God for making you in His image. You are demonstrating your appreciation for the work that He did creating a one of a kind masterpiece like you. Realizing that God placed so much value on you by making you into a unique and unrepeatable miracle is too great to fathom. In the world of art, the value of unique pieces of art is very high. That is the same way God himself sees you, hence the need to treat yourself in the way your Creator sees you. He describes us in the Bible as His own chosen, a royal priesthood. We are Royalty in His eyes so we ought to treat ourselves the way he sees us. David expresses it this way in Psalm 139:14 "*I will praise thee; for I am fearfully and wonderfully made: marvelous are thy works; and that my soul knoweth right well.*" When you begin to treat yourself with the understanding that God took his time in making you, you will allow the love of Christ to begin to flow, from Him to yourself and then others.

In as much as love is one of the greatest needs for humanity, the challenge is that we live in a fallen world where at times, those who should be present to give you love may fall short due to their own imperfections. Attributes like selfishness, jealousy, hatred are great enemies to love, and they cause the world around us to be harsh and unkind. This also shows that the love of men will always have limitations. Plugging yourself into God's love will allow you to rise from the disappointments and rejection of men, thereby flooding yourself with God's unconditional Love

'Empty Cup Syndrome'

Most people want to be sincerely present, loving and helpful to those they are close to. These relationships vary from a nuclear family level, to friends, and different areas of service in which they are engaged in the community, work or church. Most of these sacrificial acts of love being given, come from the right place because they have a genuine desire to be loving. They also have the desire to fulfill their responsibilities to those they love. The issue however arises when one is always giving and giving but does not allow time to replenish, restore or even fill themselves up again so that they are able to continue giving. When you're so focused on "giving" all the time that you don't take the time to sufficiently build up your OWN reserves. You are essentially trying to give from an empty cup. Common sense tells us that when there's nothing there, you can't give anything. Psychologists refer to this as the "Empty Cup Syndrome".

The love you give to those around can only be determined by the amount of 'Self Love' you have within you. It is unfortunate that people deprive themselves of this basic need but are still trying to give out something they themselves are deprived of. In such a case you realize that someone is battling to serve something from an already empty cup. We have heard or experienced as part of standard pre-flight announcements, the flight attendant announces that "if there should be a change in cabin pressure... put on your oxygen mask first before helping others." The main reason passengers in the plane get this instruction is that If one tries to help others first before putting on their oxygen mask one could pass out without doing any good. This is similar to what can happen when you continue to give of yourself from an empty cup. You find that some individuals are already gasping for oxygen yet they are so desperately trying to give others the already diminishing resources they have. This is fruitless kindness which will result in you being unable to function at all.

No one with a car embarks on a journey on an empty gas tank. For a car to be fully functional before the journey commences, the owner takes it for service, gets it oiled up and gassed up, enabling the vehicle to operate at its optimum capacity. It is unfortunate that people do not give themselves even just a quarter of the care they give to their cars or gadgets. They ensure their phone is charged so they can use it but don't recharge themselves. Some of us are operating on an almost empty tank, or low battery. It is just a matter of time before we knock and shut down. Self-care is the way we service or recharge ourselves so that we are able to operate at our highest capacity.

It is unfortunate however that time after time, most people are constantly trying to be all things to everyone without spending the necessary time to build themselves up first. It then becomes a weakness where you are present for everyone else except yourself. Some people tend to neglect their health, their careers, finances, mental and emotional well-being, because they are so busy taking care of everyone else around them. I'm not saying that you should become selfish or self-centered. What I am saying is that you should practice more SELF-LOVE. When you truly love yourself, you'll make your own growth and well-being a priority.

When you learn to make yourself a priority and replenish yourself when you need to, then you are sure to have sufficient reserves to give to those that you love, care about and want to help along their journey. It's very difficult for you to help or guide others if you're not taking care of your needs first. Living the best version of yourself inspires others to live the best version of themselves.

Self-care is an investment into the future. If you practice a healthy lifestyle, you are investing for a longer lifespan ensuring that you will still be present for those you love and be able to serve them fully. The better you are, the better you can be for those around you. Self-love is the way we service or recharge ourselves so that we are able to operate at our highest capacity.

How to Practice Self-Love

It is important that you treat yourself with love, care, respect and kindness from inside out. Love your soul enough to find wholeness if it's broken. Love your spirit by receiving grace, salvation and God's love. Love the body which God gave you, even with its imperfections because you will be in that body until you die. Love the crooked tooth, that scar you have, your body shape. Don't hate your body, it is yours. Nourish it and find the best way of dressing the flaws. Love your body enough to keep it in a healthy state. Exercise, watch what you eat, manage your weight to a healthy level with your Body Mass Index. Remember that your body is the temple of God, so watch who you allow access to your body and maintain your pride. When you love yourself, it shows even on the outside, you glow. Invest in yourself to be the best you can be. Teach the world how to treat you, as they will treat you the way you treat yourself. Love from other people is attracted by the love we have for ourselves

Do not entertain negative emotions like unforgiveness, bitterness, and hatred. Those emotions only hurt you, not the person/people you are bitter against. Learn to forgive yourself and treat yourself with grace. When you repent from your shortfalls, remember that there is no more condemnation to those in Christ Jesus. Our father God allows us second chances and forgives us, so receive that forgiveness and practice self-forgiveness. Acknowledge that you are only human and be confident enough to start over when you need to.

It is good for you to find your "me" time, to re-center yourself and find true joy in yourself so that you can give the best of yourself to others. Give yourself that well deserved break when you need it, at times all you need is that 30 minute "me" time. Do something you love or something that makes you happy. It is ok for you to look your best and take care of your body. Love on you, to the extent that you are irresistible to those around you. Know when you are exhausted or drained physically or emotionally and find ways of resting. When you keep saying you are ok even when you are not, people will believe you and keep piling things on you. Know even when you are in an environment that is toxic for you and preserve yourself from it by setting healthy boundaries. Love yourself and don't feel guilty about pampering yourself. I have realized some people feel bad when they do something good for themselves such as buying themselves a good meal, or that beautiful piece of clothing. Such considerations and acts of kindness to yourself are necessary to keep you nourished.

Love yourself enough to protect your dignity, love yourself enough not to sell yourself short. Set high standards for yourself and do not compromise because you are not cheap. You are the only one who can place value and a price tag on yourself. You are God's best - designer made. Love you, be you, do you, don't even try to be a copycat. You are the only one who can give the world the best version of you, so be you. Don't be under pressure to fit into groups, or a certain box. Dare to be different because you are unique.

Most characters written in the Bible made history by being different, they didn't have to fall in line with the norm, they dared to be themselves and to be different. Characters like Deborah, Samuel, Esther, Samson, David, Daniel, Peter, Paul etc, were just different and that is what made them great. Love yourself enough to arise and make your light shine. Time and again take a moment to do a self-check and ask yourself, "WHAT ARE YOU DOING TO FILL YOUR CUP?".

My Own Testimony on Self-Love

When I realized how lack of self-love was breeding so much negativity in my life, I began to take deliberate actions towards loving myself- appreciating and accepting who God made me to be. I was finding joy in Christ and realizing that God was delighted in me. I realized that I was accepted and approved by Christ, so I deserved to be loved. I began to see changes from within - so much joy and peace. The love I was giving myself from within began to show on the outside. People started asking me what had happened to me because the change could be seen on the outside. My countenance could not hide the joy bubbling from within. I noticed that people enjoyed being around me more. This is my true story - self-love is therapeutic and it can heal you from inside out. A lady friend of mine was so struck with the changes she was seeing in me that she sent me a photo grid of me telling me that she could see a great change in me. I choose to share this photograph with you because it shows a remarkable difference seen by others, yet it is the same person who chose to love herself and get plugged to the love of Christ.

After sharing my testimony with a group of ladies I had been working with on the Journey to Emotional Health, another lady from my group shared her testimony on how self-love helped bring her struggling marriage back to life again. She has given me permission to share her story.

Testimony

"The topic on self-love has helped me a lot Samu. When I read about it in the lessons you shared, I decided to implement it and it worked for me. Sometime last year my hubby had started acting funny with my house-help. Fortunately, I discovered it before they had gone far. However, when I read about self-love I decided to check on myself and discovered that I only concentrated on taking care of my children while neglecting myself. On the other hand, the maid used to dress well because she was buying new beautiful clothes for herself every time she got paid, something I was not doing. When I realized that, the following month I used almost half my salary to transform my wardrobe and started loving myself. The results of loving myself have been phenomenal. At some point my husband no longer wanted to be near me, even in church. This has since changed. He even told me that I am afraid that someone may snatch you from me, because of the way you are these days - you look beautiful. Even at work, most of my workmates have seen the changes. I used to be small built but these days I have gained a little bit of weight. My husband is now loving me and he is now the best husband. He now brings money home, we are now planning together and he respects me. I decided to continue with my house help and still live with her. As things changed she has stopped competing with me. Thank you for the lesson on self-love. I have discovered that you cannot get love from someone else if you don't

love yourself first."

Exercise on Self Love

Take time to be in touch with yourself and love you, like you have never been loved, I want you to be real about this.

I encourage you to take pen and paper as you immerse yourself in the feeling of being totally loved by yourself. Take some time to write a love letter to you. This is very important because many of us are waiting to be loved, valued and appreciated by someone else. You are however able to do this for yourself first and then allow this love to overflow to the others.

In this love letter I want you to address yourself in the best way you would ever want to be addressed, E.g. Dear Samu/ Beloved Samu

Then answer the following questions/ phrases about you

1. What I love most about you ...
2. What I value most about you ...
3. What I admire about you...
4. Thank you for being ...
5. I forgive you for ...
6. I wish....... for you.

As you do this, remember God is love and allow the love of God to flood your heart.

CHAPTER 3

DEALING WITH REJECTION

Rejection is an almost unavoidable aspect of being human. No one has ever succeeded in love or in life without first facing rejection. The need to be accepted by others stems from the pretext that love is a basic need and that all of us are born with an innate need to be accepted. The challenge arises when those you are expecting to accept you choose to reject you. In my own journey, I have realized that rejection is a major source of pain and can threaten your wholeness in a big way. The experience of rejection is ubiquitous to all humanity; it is thus safe to say that all of us will at some point experience it. It is a cross cutting experience which does not discriminate between gender, race, class or age. Rejection has the capacity to visit you at whatever stage in life and bring untold pain and emotional traumas with it.

No one is immune to rejection such that even the most perfect person that walked on this earth Jesus of Nazareth was not spared from rejection. The Bible speaks of him in Psalm 118:22 and says *"The stone that the builders rejected has become the chief corner stone"*

Isaiah 53:3 also says this about Jesus *"...He was despised and rejected of man"*.

Jesus was rejected at many levels, he was rejected by his own people and family as explained in John 1:11 *"He came to His own, and those who were His own did not receive Him."*

Jesus was rejected by the people he came to save, when Pilate presented Jesus and the robber Barabbas before the people. The people rejected him and chose Barabbas over him to be released. Judas Iscariot, one of his own disciples is the man who betrayed him and handed him over to the Romans for crucifixion. That is rejection. As if it was not enough, even Peter, who had been one of those closest to Jesus, denied him three times in one night. With all the unconditional love Jesus gave, culminating in the ultimate sacrifice of his own life at the cross, part of his narrative came from having been rejected by his own. Who are we then, to assume that we cannot be rejected?

I would like to highlight to every individual reading this, that rejection is not a new phenomenon. You are not the first nor the last to experience rejection. It is part of the journey and you need to be equipped to face it as it will come your way in life. The aim of this piece is to help you build resilience to rejection as it is an inevitable experience that any of us can go through. Most of us have already experienced rejection and carry wounds of having been rejected by those you were hoping to accept you.

In as much as we can accept that rejection is a part of the journey of life, the honest truth is that, it's impact can be more far reaching than we can imagine. Speaking in all fairness, the experience of rejection can hurt so badly. If internalized, rejection can throw you totally off balance, leaving you in severe depression, self-doubt, intense feelings of insecurity and altogether unhealthy emotionally. It can infuse feelings of fear in you, resulting in you being afraid to trust or love again. Rejection can totally derail you in life as it has the ability to wound you, leaving you hopeless with a very negative perspective to life. When you are rejected by someone, it usually eats into the way of how you value yourself, making it difficult for you to operate in the full capacity of your God-given value and purpose.

Rejection can be experienced in so many forms and relationships. It can manifest through rejection by a parent, father/mother even in-utero before one is born. Rejection can come from a lover, spouse, in-laws or relatives. You can experience rejection through failing to get a scholarship, job or political position you wanted. A group you might have wanted to be part of can choose to dissociate you, leaving you feeling unwanted. The list goes on and on, you can even add your own experience of when you felt rejected to this list.

Infection of Rejection

1Peter 5:8 says this *"Be sober, be vigilant; because your adversary the devil, as a roaring lion, walketh about, seeking whom he may devour:"*

The devil, in his mission to kill, steal and destroy, looks for opportunities to sow his seeds of negativity which can steal our joy and leave us miserable. Rejection is one tool Satan uses as it sows seeds of negativity in you, making it fertile ground for him to work in your life. It is often in those times when we are rejected, that we feel the most alone, outcast, and unwanted.

Every time you face rejection, be aware that it is a foothold of the devil because he feeds on it to attack your soul. When you experience rejection, the first feeling you get is the pain and shock of having been rejected. This pain can develop into a wound in your soul. When a person has an untreated wound on their body, it may become infected. The body will show signs that there is infection through a series of symptoms. This wound can become septic resulting in the body experiencing symptoms such as fever and general discomfort. A soul wound however, is different in that it can be hidden to those around you. You can carry soul wounds for a very long time and those around you will never know that you are hemorrhaging internally. You might be able to mask your pain behind smiles or make-up, yet there is a whole storm brewing in your soul. If a soul wound of rejection is not attended to, the pain, and hemorrhaging will not disappear, but can breed different kinds of infections which later manifest in our personality as negative/toxic traits. These toxic personality traits can in turn result in some form of dysfunction in relationships. Some infections of rejection can be detected in negative emotions like offense which can lead to bitterness and unforgiveness.

It is important to note that there are some traits of rejection which can be noticed when a person's inner wounds have not been healed. Infections of rejection are manifested over time in a person. Some examples of personality traits that stem from rejection are feelings of insecurity, low self-esteem, self-hate, anger and bitterness. Other dysfunctional personality traits that might be subtle can manifest in the form of extreme perfectionism, extreme pride, approval addiction, and excessive need to please people. You find that someone who might have been rejected can project such traits to prove that they are not what was implied by the person/people who rejected them. I mention this so that you are able to check yourself and determine if you might just be operating from a place of rejection through these seemingly acceptable personality traits.

To help explain this I will share with you a story of a friend of mine.

The first time I met her was in some public transport commute and she was in the company of her son. What perplexed me was that she was yelling at her son for having worn the wrong shirt. Later we met and became close friends and prayer partners. We had always laughed about this first time I had met her. As we prayed together, we got to a point where we were asking God to search our hearts according to Psalm 139: 34-35. God began to reveal so many things we had to act on and transform. The issue of taking offense and bitterness would always show up for us as we prayed. As we spent more time together, I began to notice these traits of extreme anger and perfectionism. She could get irritable when there was a little disorder in her home. She would always be yelling at her house help and children. As the Lord continued to work with us, these traits began to change.

After this, she began to open up and share her story with me. We realized the roots of rejection in her life, even from the time she was in the womb. She explained that when her mom discovered that she was pregnant with her, she had already packed her suitcase to go to college. She was so devastated that her dream to go to college had gone down the drain due to this pregnancy. From that moment her mum rejected her in the womb. She resented the coming of this child, because it derailed her from achieving her dreams in life. As a result, she grew up feeling rejected by her own mother. To add on to the pain she already had, her first boyfriend raped her leaving her with more pain and bitterness. All these experiences were enmeshed in her wounded soul. The Holy Spirit revealed to her that she had so much bitterness that came from rejection and she began to pursue her emotional healing.

She had come to know Jesus as her personal savior at a young age and became a powerful, anointed woman of God. Nevertheless, she still carried those unhealed wounds of rejection. This shed a lot of light for me on the fact that;
This is not always the case because people need to pay attention to their wounds and actively pursue healing of their soul. People should not confuse anointing with being whole. Anointed people can still come from broken families and experience marital breakdowns due to inner wounds they carry or some caused by others. As I grew up in church, I had thought for a long time that being in church meant families were intact and perfect. But with time I have realized that this is a myth and that growing up in church does not necessarily protect you from the wounds of rejection. In fact, the need to portray this perfection in the church can potentially breed the infection of rejection.

Another aspect to note about my friend is that in her unhealed state she was also inflicting pain on those she loved through her dysfunctional traits.

As she exhibited anger towards those around her she was in turn creating feelings of rejection in them, resulting in emotional scars on her children and others. This also demonstrates how the impact of rejection can be far reaching by creating a generational pathology of brokenness, if this cycle is not broken by getting the wounds healed. As the saying goes 'hurt people hurt others', thus creating a vicious cycle of brokenness even for generations to come. This means that pursuing your wholeness is non-negotiable for the sake of your own offspring and those you are in relationships with.

The Reaction to Rejection - The Silent Killer

When taking a closer look, you realize that so much of the hurt and struggle we endure when we have been rejected isn't even based on the rejection itself. The one major factor that magnifies the challenge of being rejected is the story we tell ourselves about the experience. It is often in our perspective and interpretation of the experience of rejection that we end up drowning in the pain. We are often our own greatest enemy through the way in which we define our rejection. Check the progression of events when one has been rejected. Think of the cruel ways in which you put yourself down, flooding the mind with thoughts of hopelessness about the future.

Most of the time when rejected, the inner critic begins to whisper into your mind. Thoughts of worthlessness and inadequacy begin to flood your mind. Some rhetoric which comes through when one has been rejected can be "I am not good enough, I am unworthy of love, I have always been a failure". Such dialogue in the mind is the story some people begin to tell themselves in the face of rejection. They established their own response to the experience and tell themselves that it is their overall reality in life.

Reaction to rejection is also based on elements and events from our past. You may begin to think of another time you were rejected and start building a case that you are not worthy. As a result, how we react to rejection is often equally or even more significant than the rejection itself. It is critical to know that there is always another perspective when bad things happen. It is the same with regards to being rejected. As you proceed on your journey, always be aware that for all that happens in Gods calendar all things are working together for your good. Even with regards to rejection, God has a way of working rejection out for your good. What is important is that you begin to tell yourself a different story from the negative chatter that has been going on in your head.

A good example is the story of Joseph, who was rejected by his own blood brothers who did the evil of selling him off as a slave and deceived his father that he had been killed. The end of the story is amazing, he ends up as Prime Minister in Egypt, and becomes the savior for his brothers who had tried to kill him before. The key is to change your story and reaction to the experience of rejection.

The quotes below provide a different perspective to rejection and are some healthy ways of understanding what you are experiencing during rejection:

- "Man's rejection is God's protection."
- "Man's rejection is God's redirection."
- "Promotion comes after rejection."
- "When a person rejects you, it is a divine announcement that they no longer have the capacity to be a blessing to you."
- "People reject you because they are not tied to your future or destiny."
- "When one door closes another door will open."

Why People Reject You

I would like to share with you some reasons why people reject you. Having this knowledge will empower you to understand the dynamics that are at work during rejection. It will help you to see rejection for what it truly is. When you see rejection for what it truly is, you will not react to the negative emotions that rejection invokes in you. This is simply because emotional reactions are never objective and have the capacity to rob you of your personal power. It is unfortunate that most us have emotional reactions to events that happen to us in life. The emotions you get from an experience are not necessarily the truth, they are merely a result of your interpretation of the event. It is important for you to be aware that when people mistreat or reject you, it is not a reflection of who you are but a revelation of who they are and their own perspective and understanding of you.

Below, are some reasons why people can reject you:

1. Rejection can be a result of another person's distorted vision and not a depiction of your value.
You realize that some people reject you because they are blind to who you truly are. Everyone is entitled to their own opinion about you, but the opinion that matters most concerning you, is the opinion of your maker, Jehovah God. This means that when one is blind to who God made you to be, they can discard and reject you. But who you are, your authentic identity, does not change because of another's distorted perception of who you are. When someone is blind to who you truly are, anything you do to try to get their approval will be fruitless. It is wise that when you Identify such characters who reject you in such a manner, that you deal with them with the understanding that the rejection is a result of their blindness and not a true reflection of who you are. It becomes easier to process their rejection when you realize

that their perception is not a true reflection of who you are. You then treat it as their perception and do not allow it to become your reality. Because that is what it is - a perception. God's perception is your true story - stick to it.

2. Rejection can be a result of your existence exposing another person's failure.

This happens a lot with parents who reject their own children. For instance, if a child came as an "accident" or unplanned pregnancy, it exposes the failure of the parent. The truth is that, this child is not responsible for their coming into the world, yet for the parent, seeing this child is a constant reminder of their mistake. They choose to ignore, deny or reject this child who reminds them of their mistakes. There are numerous cases of absent fathers, some who deny their child in utero. Some mothers can just mistreat and abuse a child that came at a time they were not ready. The story I shared of my friend who was rejected by her mother demonstrates this.

3. Rejection can also be a result of your success exposing another's failure.

At times your success and progress can expose another's fears and insecurity. Your potential and progress exposes their intrinsic inadequacies. They are threatened by your success, and as a result they choose to reject you. This happens a lot in scenarios where someone in a higher leadership position notices that someone who is subordinate to them is exhibiting a lot of potential and they have inner fears that they can be outdone, overshadowed or overtaken. They have insecurities that the younger will expose that they might not be good enough for the task in comparison to them. This can happen, in professional, religious, marital or family settings. At times the person in the superior position can use emotional abuse to trash, mistreat and justify the rejection of this person they are threatened by.

4. Some people will reject you because they are broken inside.
Hurt people hurt others, broken people break others, sad people make others sad. This is a group you will eventually have to look at with so much compassion as they need emotional healing for themselves.

How to Deal With Rejection

I trust that by now you are at a point where you can do soul searching to see if any of your personality traits are rooted in rejection. As we delve into how we can deal with rejection, there is no better example than Jesus, who went through the same challenges we face today and overcame gracefully. The rejection Jesus faced was so intense, yet his response to it was unique. He never took it to heart, neither did it stop him from doing good to others or receiving them. It is this kind of resilience that we all need to learn to help us deal with rejection.

1. The first most powerful tool that Jesus used was forgiving those who rejected him.
A very powerful statement he said while he was facing the pain of rejection on the cross was, *"Father, Forgive them **for they do not know what they do."*** Luke 23:24 (emphasis mine).

Most of the time people who reject you and cause you pain do not know what they are doing. I know that when a person is causing you pain, you believe that they know fully well what they are doing and they are intentionally causing you harm. What is important to realize is that a person who intentionally causes pain could be blinded by the evil in their heart. They are most likely carrying inner dysfunction that they are not aware of. It takes more effort and maturity for a person to be selfless and kindhearted than to do evil. When you begin to understand that, you can then agree that those who reject you and cause you pain do not know what they are doing. You are then able to look at them with compassion and repeat the words of Jesus, releasing them to God. Most times even if you tried you might not be successful in trying to reason with the person who rejected you. If they knew better, they would not mistreat people they would be loving and accepting. They truly do not know what they are doing so take it as such, practice forgiveness and let it go.

2. Accept what has happened for what it is.
Acceptance allows you to face your reality and enable you to process the hurt and pain you feel

through rejection. To cut off or brush over our feelings doesn't usually serve us when we're experiencing a painful rejection in our lives. It's important to allow ourselves to feel the sadness or anger that's stirred up in us when we feel rejected. Some of these feelings may go deeper, because they trigger old, core emotions. While we shouldn't allow our feelings to take over how we behave, we shouldn't try to shut them off entirely. We need to process the pain so that we exchange our pain for healing. Isaiah 61:3 tells us *".... To receive the beauty for ashes, the oil of joy for your mourning and the garment of praise for the spirit of heaviness..."*

Acknowledging and processing your pain is the cure for the infection of rejection. There can be no proper treatment without proper diagnosis in the medical field. This is similar to facing your pain so that you can get the soul therapy you need for your emotional healing.

3. Replace the Rejection by receiving God's love. What increases the pain of our rejection is that we have too much expectation of people. People will be people and have the potential to reject or accept you. The key is to remember what God says about you. Understand that you are accepted and approved by God. I remember a time when I had to make this saying my everyday declaration:

"Accepted By God, Approved By God, End Of Story."

I literally wrote it in many places so I could remind myself. This really brought inner healing to me. If you are ever in a lot of pain or feel overwhelmed by emotion, take your pain to God, receive God's unconditional love, and allow the Holy Spirit to heal you of the pain. Ephesians 1:5-6 puts it this way: *"Having predestined us into the adoption of children by Jesus Christ to himself, according to the good pleasure of his will, To the praise of the glory of his grace, wherein he hath made us accepted in the beloved"*

4. Seeking help in a safe place is always a wise idea.

Processing the pain alone at times can be very difficult and overwhelming. Acknowledge when you need counseling or need to talk to someone you trust. This is an important aspect of self-care. We often feel relieved when we pour ourselves to another. Counseling also opens us to new perspectives because the pain of rejection can overwhelm and diminish your ability to see things differently.

5. Don't be your own enemy by allowing your inner critic to speak louder than God's word.

Treat yourself with kindness vs self-judgment. When we notice our critical inner voice creeping in and coloring our outlook, we should aim to practice self-kindness. Essentially, we should treat ourselves the way we would a friend. When a friend comes to us with their pain, we are empathetic to them, we speak kind words to them and assure them that things will get better. We can be sensitive and empathetic to our own struggle too. Through self-compassion and love, we can be a friend to ourselves when we experience rejection.

6. Embrace and pursue your authentic identity.

Celebrate the things that make you unique and focus on things that bring happiness to you. Find ways of going back to finding your authentic identity. Stop defining yourself the way those who rejected you define you, and replace those thoughts with an unshakable understanding that God made you uniquely and accepts you that way. Replace all negative definitions of your identity with positive affirmations from God's word. Replace the lies from rejection with the Word of God you can stand on. It is possible to let go of rejection and rise above it, through speaking what you want into being, through professing the Word of God.

7. Find Purpose in your Pain.

Use the pain of rejection to grow stronger by asking God where you can see Him in the pain and any lessons He has for you through this rejection. Find purpose in your pain. Everything lies in how you choose to respond to rejection. Remember Rejection is a sign that you are pursuing new limits and not afraid to begin something new so even in the face of rejection, keep going.

CHAPTER 4

FORGIVENESS

Getting rid of Unforgiveness, Anger and Bitterness

We need to understand that we all live in an imperfect world, surrounded by imperfect people. This fact alone poses the potential for all of us to experience things that will hurt us in relationships. All of us at one point or another have had to deal with being hurt, betrayal, rejection or any such experiences. In these instances, when we have been hurt by others, we have been confronted with the need to forgive. The biggest challenge with forgiveness is that it is not always easy, especially when the pain runs so deep and the offense so severe making it very difficult for one to forgive with human power. Most of us are aware that we need to forgive, but the big question lies in 'how' we can forgive.

This chapter aims to tackle the 'how' question with regards to forgiveness, as well as highlight the benefits of forgiveness and letting go of the pain and bitterness associated with it.

Offense Is Inevitable

In Luke 17: 1-5 Jesus said this
"Then said he unto the disciples, It is impossible but that offenses will come: but woe unto him, through whom they come! It were better for him that a millstone were hanged about his neck, and be cast into the sea, than that he should offend one of these little ones. Take heed to yourselves: If thy brother trespass against thee, rebuke him; and if he repent, forgive him. And if he trespass against thee seven times in a day, and seven times in a day turn again to thee, saying, I repent; thou shalt forgive him. And the apostles said unto the Lord, Increase our faith."

As you move along on your journey to wholeness, be conscious that it is virtually impossible to live a life in which offenses will not come. This scripture indicates that it is a given and also quite normal for every human being to have experiences that will offend, hurt or bring anger. In fact, people around you will do things that have the capacity to offend you on a daily basis. Living your life with this understanding will help you to be equipped and to build resilience as and when these offenses come your way. Also, due to proximity and trust that you have built towards certain people, it is those closest to you that tend to offend you more than anyone else. The offenses you will face will vary in intensity or magnitude. What will make the difference, will be the extent of the impact and more than anything else, your response to the offense. In the scripture above, Jesus does mention that indeed there is a reward for the offender, however you should not be the one exercising punishment on those who offend you. On the contrary, Jesus instructs us rather, to 'take heed to' or 'pay attention' to ourselves. Jesus gives this instruction simply because the only aspect you have the power to change when you are offended is you - and not the other person. According to Jesus, our response should rather be to forgive those who hurt or offend us. He adds that the maximum number you should forgive one person in a day is 7x 70 times, which is a lot of times by any measure.

Understanding Forgiveness

To explain this further we will start by highlighting what forgiveness is not.

- Forgiveness is not condoning someone's behavior or saying that what a person did is right.
- Forgiveness is not excusing someone's behavior or rationalizing it.
- Forgiveness is not accepting you were wrong even when you are not by taking the blame for what went wrong.
- Forgiveness is not saying that what was done to me is ok, if you have been wronged you have been wronged and that is what it is 'wrong'.
- Forgiveness is not letting someone off the hook, but rather handing them over to the gracious hands of the almighty God.

Forgiveness is an intentional and voluntary process by which a person who has been hurt or offended undergoes a change of feelings and attitudes regarding an offense and makes a choice to release and let go of negative emotions such as vengefulness, hatred and bitterness. You need to understand that forgiveness has less to do with the other person and more to do with you.

Jesus insists that we forgive those who have offended us, because lack of forgiveness has a way of causing more harm to us the offended than the offender. When you refuse to forgive you continue to give the offender power to control how you feel and how you live your life at any given time. You give your offender the power to determine whether you are happy, sad, miserable or depressed each time you think on what they did to you. Meditating on a particular offense has a chain effect reaction which leads to feelings of anger and betrayal. This is often followed by bitterness coupled with the need for revenge or getting even. All these chain reactions are toxic tools that the devil uses to derail us from finding inner peace. In all this, God knows and acknowledges your pain, but the best promise that He gives us in this regard, is that He Himself will avenge us. The emphasis on forgiveness is because, forgiving the person who hurt you is of more benefit to you than the person who offended you. When you have forgiven, positive elements like joy and peace make you whole and emotionally healthy. Lewes B Smedes, a writer I like, made this powerful statement on forgiveness, "*Forgiveness is setting a prisoner free and finding out that the prisoner was you.*" Forgiveness is about you not allowing the future to pay for your past. Understand that forgiveness is an expanding emotion which opens you up to new positive energy, hope and realities. It stretches the uncomfortable zone of offense and allows you to experience a new peace. Through forgiveness you are releasing negative and toxic emotions that are occupying your space and opening yourself up to healthy emotions like love, joy and peace. By no means does forgiveness mean that what happened was ok, it just means you have made peace with the pain and that you are ready to let it go so that you find your wholeness and peace.

Having understood these benefits of forgiveness by no means downplays how difficult it can be to forgive. Forgiving someone who has hurt you is not easy and can be a greater challenge with those closer to you. The inner turmoil that comes with bitterness and anger is that which you need to let go,

"

Unforgiveness/ bitterness is a weight that burdens only you and not the one who hate you #emotionalhealthdairies

simply because it does not affect the one who hurt you but yourself. Understanding that forgiveness is one powerful act of self-love should motivate you to do it. You also need to forgive others so that you can be forgiven and also so that you can forgive yourself.

The Impact of Unforgiveness

One other reason why you should forgive is because the weight of unforgiveness weighs you down and puts your soul in an unhealthy place. Unforgiveness does not only negatively impact your emotional health but its impact can be so far reaching to your physical, psychological and spiritual health too. It is my hope that when you get an understanding of the extent of the damage you are inflicting on yourself by not forgiving, that you will begin to work towards forgiving and letting go of your bitterness.

*"For if ye forgive men their trespasses, your heavenly Father will also forgive you: But if ye forgive not men their trespasses, neither will your Father forgive your trespasses."*Matthew 6:14-15

"Blessed are the merciful: for they shall obtain mercy. Blessed are the pure in heart: for they shall see God."
Matthew 5:7-8 KJV

What brings us to having the confidence that we are the children of God is the simple fact that we have been forgiven by God. God's forgiveness towards us is not conditional on the size or intensity of our sins. As a matter of fact, God promises us that though our sins are red like crimson he will make them white as snow. In our day to day walk with Christ we are always so desperately in need of his mercy. Imagine if God treated us the way we really deserved, we could have been consumed. Lamentations 3:22 says *"It is of the Lord's mercies that we are not consumed., because his compassions fail not"*

Now for us to be partakers of this mercy God gives, we ought to extend this mercy to others also. Even in the Lord's Prayer, Jesus taught us to say, *"forgive us our trespasses as we forgive those who trespass against us"*. Unforgiveness hinders us from experiencing the mercy of God over our lives. It is important to understand that what God instructs us in His Word is never ever to harm or punish us, but it is to our benefit when we obey. It is God's nature to forgive and he has demonstrated this to us by sending his son Jesus as an atonement for our sin. We also need to follow suit because unforgiveness is very fertile ground for the Devil's activity in your life.

In the time you choose not to forgive, you form partnership with the enemy Satan and open the door for negative activity like anger, bitterness and hate in your soul. When we respond to hate with hate we become carriers, agents and givers of hate and embody all the baggage that comes with it. What I am saying is, you cannot give hate before it becomes a part of you, meaning that you have to become the hate before you give it. The authentic you, becomes a vessel contaminated and defiled with hateful thoughts and substances that enable you to adequately meditate on thoughts of revenge and bad wishes to the one who has hurt you. Now when you demonstrate forgiveness and love instead of hate and vengefulness you preserve your soul from defilement of hateful elements.

Another level described in the word which exemplifies this, can be found in Luke 6:38 which says *'Give, and it shall be given unto you; good measure, pressed down, and shaken together, and running over, shall men give into your bosom. For with the same measure that ye mete withal it shall be measured to you again'* Luke 6vs38

This Bible verse has been mostly quoted by preachers with regards to giving offerings in church, but it also refers to the giving of anything that you can potentially give in this life. In line with our conversation of forgiveness if you give out hate or negativity in the justification of revenge, remember that it shall be given back to you, good measure pressed down shaken together, running over shall men pour into your bosom. My prayer is that God helps us to give only the best, only the good, only the lovely so that we may be receivers of the very same things.

When people continue to do evil towards you and offend you, know that they are limited in their thinking and see them in that light. It is only God who can change a person and remove their blinkers. This means that when you forgive even when the offender never acknowledges how much they have hurt you, you actually become the bigger person who has chosen to sit with Christ in the seat of compassion and forgiveness. It is important that we learn to trust God to know what He will do with your offender and not try to put matters into your own hands.

What I am simply saying is this, unforgiveness is

toxic for you, hence you want to release this negativity by filling yourself with God's love and receiving the help to forgive and find your inner peace.

Have you ever been in a situation where you see someone who has hurt you so bad, moving on with their life, prospering and living life in abundance? God does not always treat our offender in the way we believe he/she should be treated. He has his own way of dealing with them so you realize that unforgiveness imprisons you and not your offender, it steals your joy, not necessarily that of your offender. You should take responsibility of your feelings, love yourself enough to receive peace and joy offloading your bitterness and finding joy in the Holy Ghost

Unforgiveness is a window to demonic manipulation that also hinders your fellowship with the Lord. When your heart is bitter you give room to the devil to fill your soul up with negative things such as anger and bitterness resulting in a contaminated heart before God. This contamination will disrupt you from receiving Gods love.

Due to the intensity of negative emotions that unforgiveness brings, it can also result in a variety of long-term mental health problems such as depression and Post Traumatic Stress disorder (PTSD). These mental health challenges can also nurture suicidal thoughts which could even result in loss of life. In addition to this, unforgiveness can make way for the development of other stress related health conditions such as high blood pressure, heart disease, insomnia, obesity and many other medical complications that are connected to depression. It can cause you to have a dull physical outlook and steal your beauty. Studies show that exercising forgiveness will help you shed the unnecessary weight and baggage that come as a result of bitterness. It is more relieving to forgive than to harbor unforgiveness as forgiveness brings you positive elements such as peace and joy.

The Big Question However Is "How Can I Forgive?"

In this section we will take time to discuss practical tools to help us forgive.

One of the most powerful tools to help forgive is this scripture in Matthew:
"But I say to you, Love your enemies, bless them that curse you, do good to them that hate you, and pray for them which spitefully use you, and persecute you;"
(Matthew 5:44)

This is one very tough scripture and putting it into practice cannot be done when you are operating in the flesh. The first fleshly instinct one gets when they are hurt is to be angry and look for a way to get even so that your offender feels the pain that they have caused you also. The only way to overcome operating in the flesh is by relying on the help of the Holy Spirit who is the very present help in time of need. I got this lesson at a point in my life where I was in a state of being hurt continuously by my offenders. Understanding the instruction of praying for them from a place of love and to bless them meant that I had to drop the feelings of bitterness and revenge and draw from the most powerful source of love - 'Christ' Himself, who demonstrated His unconditional love for us. That even in our sinful state He still loved us.

I remember at some point as I submitted to this scripture, that I would pray for God to bless my offenders with tears rolling down my cheeks. Initially doing this exercise was very hard for me, but as I continued to do this, it became easier and easier to pray for them. Until I came to a stage where I did it effortlessly and I would pray so earnestly and with great compassion for my offender. Although it doesn't make sense to human emotions, praying for your offender is God's way to help you release the pain. Know that God's ways are not our ways but even in the times His ways make no sense to us, He has a way of making them work for our good. As such, you need to adjust to His ways so that things work out for you.

You need to keep on praying for your offender even though it hurts at times. Continuing to pray will become easier when done consistently the way a physical exercise would become easier when done repeatedly and consistently. When you pray for those who have hurt you it doesn't necessarily mean your prayers will change them, but one sure thing is that those prayers will change you for the better. As you pray for your offender, do it with the awareness that you are regaining your wholeness. That you are exchanging your bitter feelings with God's love, God's way and overcoming evil with good. When you pray for your offender you are allowing God's light to illuminate the darkness that the pain brings. You cannot find peace while you are holding on to hard feelings like bitterness. Praying for your offender releases the offender into God's hands. Your need to revenge and get even is now God's responsibility while you focus on getting better.

Practical Steps On How You Can Forgive.

1. Choice

Remember ultimately that forgiving someone begins with making the bold choice to forgive the person who has hurt you. You choose to forgive with the understanding that forgiveness is not for the other person, but it is for your own wholeness. At this point you have reached an understanding that you cannot allow your joy to be taken away by someone who hurt you so don't continue to give your power away in such a way.

2. Acceptance

Secondly, understand that you cannot change what happened to you in the past. What happened, happened, meaning that it is necessary to accept the fact that you cannot change this event. Sometimes what imprisons us, is an inner wish that what happened should have never happened. This relentless wish and constant reminiscing on what could have been, will not change the past because the truth is that it happened. Now facing this truth, accepting it and giving up hope that you can change the past helps you to release and say 'it is what it is'. The important thing is to understand that what you have the power to change is your now and your future, so that is what you would rather focus on.

3. Process your Pain

I have learnt that forgiveness is a process, it is a journey that requires that you allow yourself time to process your experience and emotions. The feelings of pain that come through offense cannot just be buried or forgotten, they need processing. Dealing with pain is not letting go, like just dropping something from your hand. It means coming to terms with your pain and how the event impacted you. It can be likened to when you have a wound, it needs to be nursed so that it begins to heal. Psalms 143:3 puts it this way *"He heals the brokenhearted and binds up their wounds."* Binding up their wounds demonstrates a treatment process. I remember a time when my little sister got scalded with hot water. She literally had to be taken to the clinic every day so that the wound could be cleaned and dressed. It is the same with emotional wounds, they need to be treated in a similar fashion. The size of the wound would also determine the length of time it would take to heal. There are those moments when God can do an instant miraculous healing of wounds in extra ordinary encounters with His presence. Whichever way God heals your wounds, it is important that you are open to God's nursing through the Holy Spirit.

A lot of people struggle with this part of processing the pain, because this process often hurts. Most people would rather ignore the wounds and carry on as if nothing happened. The challenge with this stance is that an emotional wound that is ignored does not go away, it will continue to settle in parts of your soul. The wound will eventually breed infections that will be transformed into toxic personality traits. Most people struggle with processing the pain because it requires opening up of the wound and this can be painful. It can be likened to when a physical wound is opened up for cleaning and dressing, it will hurt, but must be done so that no infection develops until the wound is healed. In this processing the key is to engage the Holy Spirit in everything you do because it cannot be done in human strength.

4. Pray for your offender

I explained earlier how praying for the offender opens you up to the working of God. As you do this in obedience to God you are allowing God's way of replacing darkness/evil with good. Darkness goes away by introducing light and in those moments of praying for your offender, you overcome the negative emotions of pain, anger and bitterness with the good. This will invite God's presence and assistance as you pursue your healing.

5. Counseling

At times, the emotions of pain can build up in you and will need to be released in a safe environment for you to process them. It is important that you don't bottle your feelings and emotions but instead find a safe place to vent and release what you are feeling inside. When painful emotions are bottled in, they have a way of erupting in most unwelcome moments such as uncontrolled outbursts of rage or anger. These outbursts can be embarrassing, and you would rather avoid them at all costs. Sometimes all you need, is to talk to someone who can help and counsel you during the process. Talking to someone provides release and helps you to see things differently, different options and perspectives on how to deal with your pain. Being assisted by a counselor on your healing journey is a safe way of releasing the pain inside you.

6. Journaling

Writing down your feelings on paper is another way that can help you process your pain. As you put things on paper it can help you really understand where your issues are, as well as present a safe place to vent. You can be totally honest on paper unlike when you are sharing with someone. After journaling you can lay your paper before God in prayer and receive His help to forgive and let go. Lay it all at the cross as Christ is waiting to carry the pain for you. It's amazing what relief can come from a journaling session

7. Self-Love

Another powerful act when forgiving is to extend love and compassion to yourself. Often times offenses such as betrayal, rejection and infidelity can destroy a person's self-belief and esteem. In such scenarios It's easy to start entertaining thoughts such as *'you are not good enough'* or *'you are not beautiful enough'*. We need to take care of ourselves, so that we do not take people's actions too personally. A person's actions, especially with regards to acts like infidelity have everything to do with their own lack of self-respect and self-control. This does not have a bearing on who you are, so you need to remind yourself of who God says you are. Your true identity before God never changes because of someone else's actions and disrespect of you.

Find the healing you need through receiving Gods love and in turn extending that love to yourself. There is so much power in positive affirmations that declare who God says you are every day. Doing these affirmations reminds you that you are who God says you are and also that you are accepted and loved by God in spite of the ways in which others have hurt you or treated you. Every time you have a negative thought in your mind about yourself, replace it with positive confessions and deliberately do things that bring you joy. Find time to make yourself a priority by doing things that bring you joy, such as treating yourself like the king or queen you really are. Don't entertain negative thoughts or wallow in pity parties because you give room to the devil, who capitalizes on these negative emotions to drown you in sorrows. Also check your company and ensure that you spend time with positive people and stay away from negative energy. Take full responsibility for your happiness and pursue the joy of the Lord at all times. Loving yourself will allow love to flow to you and bring you healing that will help you release the pain and forgive.

As you daily practice these actions and time progresses, you will see yourself gradually letting go of negative emotions that bring you pain. Forgiveness is a journey but God instructs us to forgive and He knows we are able to do it. All we need is to rely on His help throughout the process bearing in mind that each of our journeys are unique as we surrender to the guidance of the Holy Spirit during the process.

Is It Possible To Forgive Someone Who Is Not Sorry Or Does Not Change Their Behavior?

There are so many people who are stuck between a rock and a hard place because they have been so wronged and betrayed by others. You look at your offender and you see that they are not sorry or don't seem to even get how much they have hurt you. For some it is that situation where the person continues to hurt you. This is a very difficult place to be, where one can find it hard to forgive due to an inability on their part to look beyond the offense. One might be stuck in thinking that what went wrong should never have happened and find it hard to move from that point.

The key is to always remember that whenever you choose to forgive the impact of forgiveness is more on you than on the person that is to be forgiven. You are the one who is suffering the pain and the hurt and carrying this heavy burden so you will need to hasten to offload this burden and to let go of the pain. This can be done regardless of whether the person is sorry for their actions or chooses not to change their bad behavior. Be reminded also that when you forgive someone it does not mean that you are condoning their bad behavior. In as much as it is part of earthly experience to be offended, it is never ok when people hurt you, more so when they do it repeatedly. In-fact, it is selfish and inconsiderate behavior on their part. That being said, remember also that you have no power to change another person and the only person you can change is you and not them.

The other thing about forgiving someone is understanding that their bad actions have nothing to do with you. I have had to learn that I shouldn't take people's actions so personally and to remember that some people hurt you from the place of their own brokenness and dysfunction. This means that their actions are a reflection of the dysfunction inside them. When you begin to understand that, you leave your offender with his/her baggage and do not allow yourself to carry their baggage by accepting their pain and making it yours. That is why you need to let it go, because you know forgiveness is for your own good and emotional health. Now when a person continues to hurt you in this way it reflects that they carry problematic emotional baggage, which you don't have the power to change.

Their bad behavior does not remove the fact that forgiveness is of more benefit to you.   Extending forgiveness to them remains non-negotiable for your emotional health and peace. A big challenge some people have is that they mistake forgiveness as letting someone off the hook for their bad behavior. When you have forgiven and handed over the issue to God, you need to trust God to handle your offender. He will avenge on your behalf in his own way, which may not necessarily be your way.

Now for an ongoing relationship, it is necessary for both parties to take responsibility for their actions so that a healthy relationship ensues. The Bible tells us to "guard our hearts with all diligence for from it flows the issue of life." Part of loving yourself includes guarding your heart from someone you can see is willfully hurting you. By this I mean when someone continues to hurt you repeatedly, at some point there needs to be a system put in place that helps you guard your heart. When you guard your heart it does not mean that you don't forgive them but it simply means you come to a point where you set up boundaries and an immunity line that requires the perpetrator to take responsibility for their actions if they want the relationship to work. Boundaries will help ensure that you are respected and considered resulting in a healthy relationship.

There are times you will need to stand up and demand that you are considered in the relationship and communicating boundaries in a healthy way is a good place to begin.

Depending on the level of your resilience, it would be safe to create a system of boundaries and accountability that keeps you both in check. In the event that the boundaries you have placed are violated, there should be consequences for the offenders' actions. Someone who continues to cross the boundaries demonstrates that they have no value for you and the relationship. When there are repeated violations of these boundaries, you can choose to love those who have hurt you from a distance. Setting up boundaries needs one to develop skills of healthy communication and I have dedicated a chapter to setting healthy boundaries from a place of love.

Whatever you do in such scenarios, allow yourself to be led by the Holy Spirit and be prayerful and seek clear instructions and directions from God. I have met people who have been helped by God and have built powerful resilience who were able to handle toxic relationships and fully emerged victorious in the relationship. There is help and grace for this, I have seen God transforming unhealthy relationships, restoring them and making them healthy again through the determination of just one person to make a relationship work.

Forgiveness and Reconciliation

In the process of forgiveness, reconciliation is encouraged but is not a requirement. As such, one needs to be clear that there is a difference between forgiveness and reconciliation. Reconciliation means that a relationship is restored and the two continue with the relationship they had before an offense had taken place. There is the offender who refuses to change their behavior and continues to hurt you or pose danger to you. This person does not have to continue to have the right to access your life.

Even when God deals with us, He has set up a system where we have a responsibility to uphold His statutes and commands. In the event that we don't obey his instructions, there are consequences to be faced. For example, when Adam and Eve ate the forbidden fruit, there were consequences for these actions. It didn't mean that God did not forgive them or loved them less. It is the same with us and the people who offend us, we have a responsibility to create boundaries because the Bible instructs us to "guard our heart with all diligence for from it are the issues of life." When you see an offender threatening your issues of life by continuing to endanger and bring harm to you, you have to preserve your soul. In such cases, it is ok to forgive and love from a distance as stated previously.

Reconciliation is one powerful tool which Jesus demonstrated by which He restores us back to Him. For reconciliation to occur, the other party must be willing to make a commitment to make the relationship work. It cannot be forced on anyone, but should rather be a choice they make and a commitment on their part to abide by healthy conduct that makes a relationship wholesome. In cases where you want to consider reconciliation, take time to consider these three factors for reconciliation.

1. Conviction: you want to see if your offender feels convicted about what they did and that they are taking responsibility for what they might have done wrong to you.

2. Contrition: you want to see that the offender is humble and is truly sorry about what they did.

3. Change: they must demonstrate that their apology is not just lip service but that they have changed their wrong behavior.

In light of this, be aware that it is still possible for someone who has built up resilience to continue in a toxic relationship, even when there is no sign that a person has changed. With time, they can find grace to transform and heal the relationship through the power of the Holy Spirit. The Bible refers to such people as those who can pass through the valley of Baca (a very dry and harsh place) and are able to turn it into a spring of water. *"Blessed is the man whose strength is in thee; in whose heart are the ways of them. Who passing through the valley of Baca make it a well; the rain also filleth the pools."*

Psalms 84:5-6 KJV. What becomes very important is for an individual to have a very close relationship with the Holy Spirit who will guide you on what direction to take in a relationship as you journey to forgiveness.

Forgiving Yourself

Even after we've grasped that forgiveness is a good thing and frees us from bitterness and anger, isn't forgiving ourselves often more difficult? When we have done something we regret or made a mistake that costs us something we want, this gives power and the voice to the self-critic in us, creating feelings of guilt, shame and inadequacy. The key is to overcome the feelings of guilt and shame by realizing that who you truly are is not measured by your mistakes or your past experience.

Your significance is not rooted in those things, your significance and value has already been established by God. You are who God says you are and that should be the point of departure in forgiving yourself.

Romans 8:1 says *"There is therefore now no condemnation to those which are in Christ Jesus, who walk not after the flesh but after the spirit"*. The devil wants you to be stuck in that place where you are condemning yourself for what you did. He knows that your ability to forgive others is connected to your ability to forgive yourself. As a result, he will keep you in a vicious cycle where you fail to forgive yourself making it

> *There is a difference between where you've been, what you have done, what has happened to you and what you truly are.*

difficult to forgive others

The devil wants you to be unforgiving, always recalling and reminiscing on what so and so did to you. You keep a little black book in your heart and mind with records of how much people have wronged you and you keep recalling the sin. The truth is that the person you have written in the black book is yourself because one day you will also sin and do wrong and it will be hard to go past those scripts in the little black book to the place of forgiving yourself. The failure to forgive will create a host of negative feelings in you, turning you into your greatest critic and worst enemy.

This validates the importance of giving grace to others when they do you wrong and forgiving them such that when you fall short, you are able to forgive yourself and show the grace you would give others to yourself. You should be wary of partnering with Satan as an accuser of brethren who constantly reminds others of the wrongs they did to you. During the times you fail to forgive, the devil is nurturing a seed in you, so that in the times when you do wrong, the fruit from the seed he has sown in you, of being an accuser will start to germinate. This will result in you accusing yourself and constantly reminding you of your wrongs. Choose to be a forgiving person and minister grace to others so that you can minister grace to yourself in the moments you will need it.

CHAPTER 5

FINDING PURPOSE IN THE PAIN – (PIP)

Dealing with pain- another perspective to pain.

As I begin this chapter, it is my assumption that the bulk of us have experienced pain and challenges at some point in our lives. In the unlikely event that you haven't, I assure you that as life has it, painful experiences will come your way. You can't expect life to be 100% obstacle free simply because you are cultivating positivity. Indeed, sadness, remorse, frustration, and stress are often natural (and healthy!) responses to the ordinary losses and struggles of human life.

The Bible many times shows that hardships, difficulties and suffering are part of the human journey as shown in scriptures below;

"Yea though I walk through the valley of the shadow of death I will fear no evil for thou art with me." Psalms 23vs4

"I will be with thee; and through the rivers, they shall not overflow thee: when thou walkest through the fire, thou shalt not be burned; neither shall the flame kindle

Now appreciating that pain in the journey of life is inevitable, it therefore means how you respond to these difficulties is what will determine whether you are emotionally healthy or not. Being emotionally healthy does not mean you are delusional about the pain you are going through. It means that you have the ability to come up from under the negativity and are able to take charge of your thoughts whilst constantly reminding yourself that God is still in charge. Today I am offering an alternative perspective to aid understanding of our painful experiences that will leave you emotionally healthy and in a more peaceful, positive state.

Finding Purpose in My Pain

I recall myself being in so much pain and confusion at one point in my life. I was carrying my first baby, and at almost 7 months into the pregnancy, I unexpectedly experienced a severe case of pregnancy Induced hypertension also clinically known as preeclampsia. After the Doctor had tried everything to lower my blood pressure, he recommended that they immediately take the baby out. He explained to me that in such complicated cases, their aim would be to save mother first and then baby. I battled to process this news which I was not at all mentally or emotionally prepared for as events progressed very quickly from the moment I received this news. I remember not even knowing how to pray in that moment and simply resorted to singing the song

"You are faithful oh Lord" in my heart. After the C-section we unfortunately learnt that the baby had already been severely affected by the condition while in the womb and she did not make it. The pain of walking out of the hospital with a wound to nurse and no baby in my hands was one I still cannot describe until today.

God was faithful enough to restore what I had lost, and a year later I was joyful to hold a beautiful baby girl in my own hands. After this miraculous recovery my husband and I were once again confident to try again. Little did I know that I would unexpectedly lose another baby boy to the same condition - preeclampsia. Only this time it appeared in the earlier stages of my pregnancy.

Discouragement hit me hard again, coupled with fear that this would be my story for the rest of my life. It was a difficult journey, choosing to trust God again being aware that the risk of something like this happening again was very high. It took guts to trust God and keep declaring that God will carry me safely through another pregnancy until delivery. Thoughts of fear would often visit me, voices in my head reminding me that "last time you prayed and declared the word, but you still lost". By God's grace, I kept trusting God, talking above my fears at times like a crazy woman just to fight the fears within. God being God, after that loss, he was gracious enough and I again held in my arms another beautiful baby girl. I was crazy enough to trust God again, that I would try for the last time, asking for Him to restore the son I had lost. At that point I had to change my doctor because he had sternly warned me not to try again lest the unfortunate would happen again and take even my life. God in his faithfulness did it again and honored my request. Now I am a joyful mum of two beautiful girls and one handsome and incredible boy.

This journey I traveled was in no way an easy journey, the pain of the losses was intense. I recall times I would just wake up and sob because I didn't know what to do with the grief and pain. Amazingly, the joy of seeing God coming through for me beyond the pain, brought so much joy and purpose in my life. Little did I know, as I was going through the pain that years later, I would be a joyful mum of 3 and would walk with so many other women on their challenges related to my experience. The ability to be present for the many women who have had similar experiences, is one I could not have gotten without having gone through that pain myself.

I had to learn so many things during the journey, especially trusting God even when it didn't make sense. I also learnt that, eventually all things including our pain will work together for good. The value I have for my precious kids is something I am also grateful for. Through this experience I now know that we should never stop trying even when fear is roaring at us. Had I known the end of my story during my losses I would have never drowned myself in sorrow the way I did. I have realized that no matter what you are going through, God has a good plan for your life and you need to just trust him enough to see you through.

Joseph is one such person who went through a painful journey, being rejected by his own brothers who even tried to kill him. It is those same people who sold him off as a slave to the Egyptians whom he later on helped when he was now the Prime Minister of Egypt. Joseph's story clearly demonstrates that the journey to the fulfillment of our God ordained purpose is not always a rosy one. Even when he had begun to be favored as a slave in Potiphar's house and he was seeing hope for his future, the wife of Potiphar did the unthinkable by framing him for rape. He eventually spent years in prison, after which he got out when he miraculously interpreted Pharaoh's dream which led to his promotion in all of Egypt. During this time when he was now president, his brothers came to Egypt in need of food supplies due to the devastating famine. After all that had happened Joseph had this to say, *"But as for you, ye thought evil against me; but God meant it unto good, to bring to pass, as it is this day, to save much people alive."* Genesis 50:20

All the pain that Joseph had gone through, God had meant it to result in good and that was the significance of his painful journey. The ultimate purpose for his elevation that had been preceded by a series of painful experiences, was to save the lives of many people and those of his family. This signifies the importance of having the correct perspective to pain while we are going through it. God always has a bigger plan and agenda for us through our seasons of pain.

The major challenge is that, at times pain can have a shattering effect on us and can create an image of a hopelessness and a bleak future in the moment of pain. Think of the moments Joseph was rejected by his brothers and the pain of serving time in prison for a crime he hadn't committed. Going through those experiences couldn't have been easy for him. The negative thoughts, emotions and trauma that he had to survive during this painful phase of his life must have been very tough for him. The experience of pain and struggles we face can literally throw us off guard and flood us with a lot of negative emotions like sadness, grief, depression, bitterness, loneliness, suicidal thoughts, and at times lead to physical illnesses.

I believe however, that gaining a different perspective to the pain we are going through can alleviate the level of pain one is experiencing or rather make it bearable. You are able to go through the pain in a more hopeful state and can even draw strength from the experiences. Going through pain and finding purpose in your pain brings a new level of hope and positivity in your journey. Romans 5:3-5 says this about our pain; *" 3 And not only so, but we glory in tribulations also: knowing that tribulation worketh patience; 4And patience, experience; and experience, hope: 5And hope maketh not ashamed; because the love of God is shed abroad in our hearts by the Holy Ghost which is given unto us."*

Now when I look back at a lot of the pain that I had to go through in my life, I see that it has made me so relevant. I am able to share all this on emotional health, because I have had my fair share of pain and have managed to draw a lot of lessons from it, which I then share with others.

When you go through the pain and allow God to work in you during your pain, you will see a greater joy that lies ahead. Most amazing and beautiful things are birthed in pain. For a woman to hold a baby, she has to experience discomfort for 9 months and then pain in delivery, until she experiences the joy of motherhood. For a beautiful butterfly to be released, it needs to break out of being a hideous caterpillar. Even Jesus Christ our Lord had to suffer and go through pain so that we may have abundant life. He saw the joy that was ahead even in his time of pain. The Bible explains that he broke his body for us at the cross. It was from that place of brokenness that a new and amazing life was birthed for us.

> *Spaces of brokenness and pain are God's workshops to birth good things for us*

Based on this understanding and actions of Jesus, I have learnt that as we grieve during our painful experiences, we should allow God's purpose to be revealed. When His purposes for our pain are revealed, we are able to go through the pain with a new perspective and a different attitude. Below, are a few practical steps that can help you change your attitude to your painful experiences.

Changing Your Perspective to Pain

1. Ask the right questions

You find that most of the time when people are in pain, the question they usually ask is "why me?". It is in those moments of stress and trauma that people begin to question the occurrence of events that are unpleasant. Surprisingly when good things happen to us and we are blessed we never sit down to ask, 'why me?' Asking this question when faced with a difficult time has never made the situation we are faced with any better, on the contrary it will only intensify your grief and foster feelings of victimhood. To change this, you need to begin to ask different and more intelligent questions that create a victorious outlook to your situation. I have listed below questions that can help you process your painful experience in a healthier fashion and enable you to see another perspective to your painful experiences.

2. What does God want me to learn through this experience?

In as much as difficult times are not something we look forward to or anticipate, the truth is, there are some important lessons in life that we can only learn through the difficult times. Often times these lessons can become the silver lining in the darkness and our moments of pain. There are some things you can only learn in the storm, such as your resilience and strength, which are often revealed during times of hardship. New wine comes out of the crushing and the pressing, and gold is refined through the fire. This is what hard times do for us, they refine us and bring forth a better version of us when we allow them to do so. It is also in these times of hardship that our character is built, as life can humble you and point you to the things that really matter. Difficult times tend to turn our worlds upside down and anything that is not nailed down to the floor will go flying. It is through such an experience that you are able to see and separate between the things that really matter in life. It is only when you are at rock bottom that you gain skills to climb the mountain back up to the top. These are valuable life-skills you need in order to navigate through life and overcome challenges.

3. What Is The Godly Purpose For This Experience?

God is also present during our times of pain so that His purposes are revealed and fulfilled. When you have a painful experience and eventually conquer, you have already created a manual for the roadmap to victory for that challenge you have faced, which you can in turn share with others who go through difficult situations similar to yours. God is able to use your experience to minister direction, comfort and hope to others. It is easier for you to be present for someone who is going through something you have experienced yourself, because you understand their pain and can relate to challenges they are facing, as well as show them that there is hope for them. In the season of pain, ask God what His purpose is for that experience. When He reveals it, you are able to go through the pain knowing you will accomplish God's purposes for your life and this will bring joy and a sense purpose for you. We have seen huge ministries and organizations being formed after a painful experience. God is actually getting you ready for something bigger that he has in store for you. Someone wrote this powerful statement that now carries me through tough times, - *"One day you will tell your story of how you've overcome what you are going through now, and it will become someone else's survival guide"*

God is the revealer of purpose, so go to Him and ask Him to reveal His purpose to you during that time. Another thing to be aware of in your quest for purpose, is that a similar experience can have different meanings for people so find God's purpose for your scenario. An example is how the death of Uzziah for Isaiah was so that he sees and experiences God. Whereas for Mary and Martha the death of their brother Lazarus was so that God's glory would be seen when Christ raised him from the dead.

4. How Can God Be Seen And Glorified Through This Experience?

When you go through hardships, know that this is

an opportunity for God's intervention, so we should anticipate Him to do the miraculous for us. It is often from situations of our greatest pain that the greatness of God can be seen so that he is glorified. The greatness of God is seen through Him coming through for us in our hard times. I am reminded of the time when the children of Israel were faced with the Red Sea, while the Egyptians pursued them from behind. The people cried out to Moses in despair as they saw no hope in sight. The only place Moses could look up to, was to God Almighty for help, who in His great might and power parted the Red sea for them to cross, and also drowned the Egyptians in that sea. This was an incredible miracle which was performed at a time of great anguish and pain for the children of Israel. Lazarus had to be dead for four days so that God could be glorified through his resurrection.

- You cannot experience the healer if you have never been sick.
- You cannot experience the provider if you have never lacked.
- You cannot experience the comforter if you have never been through grief.

When you begin to view your pain as an opportunity for God to work, you begin to trust Him that all things are working for your good, no matter how bad they may seem. Remember this, that the greater the pain, the greater the miracle.

5. What Is It That I Can Be Thankful For? -An Attitude of Gratitude

A thankful heart will help shift your focus from the things that are not going your way to the blessings that you have around you. When you begin to count your blessings, your eyes are opened to how much you have been blessed and you even realize that there are some who are having it worse than you. It is all about shifting the focus because what you give attention to, will grow.

As we wrap up on Finding Purpose in Pain, it is my hope that we are feeling a little more positive about the challenges surrounding us. I recall having this discussion with my sister and she said, *"each and every one of us in life have our piece of yummy cake as well as a piece of a bitter cake in life."* Meaning that there is no one who walks upon the face of the earth and does not have that one thing that is a thorn in the flesh. There is no one immune to challenges or things that will bring you pain. It does not matter how rich they are or how blessed you think they are, there is that one area for you that will irk you. God in his grand plan, designed that we will always need him. Think about it - if all was 100% fine for you, your quest for God would not always be relentless.

In the Bible we read about Paul, who had to go to God three times about a thorn that he had in his flesh and God responded to him by telling him that "His grace was sufficient for him." What I am simply saying is that a key purpose of pain and challenges in our lives is to help us to stay connected to God. Imagine going through life and never getting to a point where you have no need for Gods intervention. God always loves to show up in our lives and come through for us, therefore challenges are an opportunity for him to show His might in our lives. This means we have to totally trust him and depend on him to meet us at our point of need. Going through pain with this understanding allows you to have an expectation for the miraculous in your life. You are then able to ask the right questions like we mentioned here and find out what God wants you to learn.

I want to encourage you, do not despair, crash or crumble when trouble comes your way. At times, all you need is to BE STILL AND KNOW THAT HE IS GOD. Don't allow yourself to stress over things you cannot change, rather hand them over to God. Worry and stress have never changed your situation. It is true that some situations can be so bad, like the one where the Israelites were faced with the Red Sea while Pharaoh's army was following right behind them. In such scenarios all you have to do is stand still to see God opening the Red Sea for you. After the storm in your life you will look back and see how things which were meant for evil will turn out for the good.

After a lady friend of mine had gone through serious challenges in her marriage and emerged victorious on the other side, she had these words to say about her ordeal, *"I thank God for the pain I went through, because I* emerged a better woman. I learnt how to do spiritual warfare and overcome. I thank God for my husband, for all the times he mistreated me, I learnt what it means to love unconditionally, I learnt patience, I learnt to be kind even to those unkind to me. I am happy with the woman I have become and I wouldn't exchange my trials for anything, because I love the woman I have become"

I thought these words were very profound and they made me see pain and challenges in a different way. You can even find at times, that you can be busy trying to change people or situations that God is using to change you.

CHAPTER 6

BOUNDARIES

For a very long time, I thought that one of the attributes of being a good Christian was allowing people free play to do as they wish in my life. With time, I ended up with a buildup of massive resentment and very miserable to the point where I realized that I had allowed and unknowingly trained people to disregard me and treat me in the way they did. I learnt that I am the owner of my space and have the responsibility to teach people how to behave in my space. It was very liberating when I became bold enough to step up and enforce boundaries in my relationships. This was a huge step in regaining my emotional health.

This is a very difficult topic to discuss in some Christian circles, as there is a perception that to be Godlike is synonymous with allowing people the freedom in and out of your life as and when they wish. I would like to dispel this myth, because even though God our father has given us so much liberty from the beginning of time, he set boundaries on how far Adam and Eve had to go in the garden of Eden. When they violated the boundary, there were serious consequences for everyone involved. The ten commandments He gave through Moses which were prefixed with 'Thou shall not', were a powerful foundation of boundaries God gave for how far we should go as his people. Even our Master Jesus in all his humility and meekness, had areas which were "no-go areas" and in no uncertain terms ensured those boundaries were respected. That one place was the temple, 'His Father's house' where he had to turn the tables upside down and use a *sjambok* to drive out people who were misusing his Father's house for selling and exchange of goods.

It is interesting to see how even with regards to nature, God separated the water from the land and set a boundary on how far the water can go. Always, when nature goes haywire and these boundaries are violated through natural disasters like tsunamis, cyclones and floods, there is untold destruction, pain and chaos. When you take a closer look at the times God set boundaries, you realize that they were always to protect us. Adam and Eve were preserved from death as long as they had not eaten of the forbidden fruit. Their disobedience resulted not only in their demise, but that of all humanity. When boundaries are violated it always results in untold pain and suffering, likewise in relationships it is important to always be on guard because violated boundaries will cause emotional pain.

Seeing that Jesus took drastic action on those who violated the sanctity of the temple really opened my eyes to the need to enforce personal boundaries. According to Him, people had pushed the boundaries way too far, turning a house of prayer into a marketplace! But isn't this what people have a tendency to do even in relationships? Due to the selfish nature of people, they are always scheming and trying to push boundaries to see how far they can go for their selfish gain. At times this is an unconscious act, much in the same way that a child will always study to measure how far they can get away with mischief before they get a spanking or time out. Some children become uncontrollable simply because there aren't any restrictions and boundaries in the home. They do what they want and always get their way. It is important to train children from a young age about the importance of boundaries and how they are there to protect them. Some people are operating from a place of dysfunction because they were never trained boundaries.

This is similar to what happens in relationships, be it romantic, family, friends or colleagues. People are always pushing these boundaries. One powerful speaker called Iyanla Vanzat said this in an interview she had with Oprah Winfrey "*People violate you when you don't have clear boundaries, because you don't tell them how to behave in your life, they run amok, they run amok because you don't have clear boundaries*"

On your journey to emotional health, it is important to take stock of your relationships with people. Some relationships you have with certain people weigh you down to the extent of causing emotional pain at times. These are toxic relationships which need you to re-evaluate issues around boundary violations in your interactions. When you search deeper in those relationships you will most likely discover that there are some boundaries that have been crossed. As you take stock of these relationships, you also need to bear in mind that no relationship is immune to conflict and disagreement. These elements actually make a relationship stronger as the demonstration of love, forgiveness and reconciliation build stronger relationships. What I am talking about here is continual monitoring, willful hurt and negativity that some people bring.

There are times you need to love yourself enough to stop people from misbehaving like what Jesus did with the traders in the temple. The Bible says in Proverbs 4vs 23, *"Guard your heart with all diligence for from it are the issues of life."* When you realize there is a threat to the flow of the issues of life, you need to put the guards in place through setting boundaries that will protect you from harm's way. Be alert in relationships, wise as a serpent and at the same time harmless as a dove.

It is not everything that people request of you that you should say yes to. It is actually more Christian to respond with a NO than to say yes and then grumble in your heart while doing the favor. Continuing to allow things to happen against your wishes in relationships will build up resentment and bitterness in you. The key to setting boundaries is in learning how to effectively communicate when you sense that your personal boundaries are being violated. Learning to say "NO" with much grace to the hearer can ease communication of boundaries. There are people who are not used to hearing "no" and will not respond well to your NO's. That is also ok, because people who are really for you and are routing for your rise might be disappointed in your NO, but because they have genuine love for you, they will understand.

There are people you might no longer allow access to your life due to their behavior, this does not mean you don't love them or that you do not forgive them, but that you realize that loving them from afar will benefit you more. When God set the boundaries for Adam and Eve it wasn't because he loved them any less. Even though there were consequences for their actions, God continued to pursue a relationship with mankind.

When I think of boundaries it reminds of a funny story that happened when we were growing up in our home with my siblings. At some point we had this "out of order" house help who had lived with us for many years. Due to familiarity she began taking my mum for granted, being disobedient, talking back and disrespecting her. To accurately describe the situation, she was now actually just running amok. My mum being the kind lady she is, even though the maid took her kindness for granted, continued to let her do whatever she wanted. At some point my sisters and I told mum to fire this house help and then she woke up one morning and told her to pack and go. This maid literally refused to be fired and to go, she told my mum in our language that *"moda kuti ndiendepi mhamha hazviite kuti mundidzinge,"* (translated - *where do you want me to go I ain't going anywhere*). Imagine that my mum failed to fire her at that point and that's what people do when you don't set firm boundaries. They will take advantage of your kindness and disregard you in ways you can never imagine,

If you want to continue in pain, live a life without boundaries and you will expose yourself to serious abuse. There is a time when you have to say NO, and place serious consequences for your boundaries to be respected. Healthy boundaries are an act of self-love, a gift of wholeness and peace of mind to yourself. It is important to teach people how to treat you and how to behave in your personal space. For as long as they observe that you are ok with what they are doing, they tend to continue or even take it a notch higher. The key is to be firm in setting these boundaries as well as enforcing them.

Another interesting example that struck me on setting boundaries in the Bible was how Sarah felt that she was now being taken for granted in her space by her maid servant Haggar who she had given to Abraham to have a son for her before she got Isaac in Genesis 21:8- 12. Sarah realized that Haggar was now despising her and said it was high time Hagar & her son had to leave her household. This was a complex but bold decision Sarah had to make for her peace and God supported her in enforcing this boundary by telling Abraham to grant Sarah's wish. When we set boundaries, we should always be led and helped by the Holy Spirit so that it is not just our misguided emotions at play. God was in support of Sarah's decision as hard as it was. Eventually his good plan of making a nation out of Ishmael the son of the bond woman was fulfilled. In the end it was a win-win situation for both parties. Indeed, some boundaries may be hard to enforce but if led of the spirit will result in the greater good for all.

It is key to be led by the Holy Spirit in setting boundaries. In listening to the leadership of the Holy Spirit, understand that He directs you in a way and language you understand. Sometimes it is that gut feeling you have inside. Pay attention to that inner voice or uneasy feeling you are having about something or someone. Sometimes you have this feeling that something is not right in a relationship. Most times the Holy Spirit is nudging you that there are boundaries being overstepped in your life.

A friend of mine once shared this story with me that she had a very close friend for a very long time in her life and they had always been friends even together with her husband. There however came a time when her friend began to get very close to her husband as she was seeking counseling. At first, my friend was ok with the situation and continued to welcome her to seek advice from her hubby. The friend began to become very close to her hubby, going for lunch meetings, calling him and meeting ever so often. Inside her she was feeling uneasy about the scenario but was finding it very difficult to set the boundaries. She did hint to hubby that she was no longer comfortable and he was just telling her that she was insecure. The lady friend continued to unprecedented levels, visiting her home when she knew that her friend would be traveling and she would be left with her husband. This was the time she realized that her kindness to her friend was now allowing her to violate boundaries. She eventually had the guts to tell her friend that she was not happy about her behavior and set boundaries. Obviously, the friend was very upset as she was benefiting emotionally from spending time with this lady's husband and she did not take the boundary that had been set very well.

When my friend shared this with an elderly lady from church, she told her that being a Christian does not mean you have to be naive and allow people to abuse your kindness in such ways.

She gave this example about Sarah, Abraham and Hagar. I am simply saying that at times setting boundaries needs boldness as well as handing the issue over to God. Allowing people to run amok in your life is to your detriment and adversely affects your emotional wellbeing.

It won't be easy to set boundaries but doing so will benefit your emotional sanity and wellbeing. At times setting boundaries is simply saying "no" to people you have always said "yes" to. At times it means saying "not now," or "I can't make it today, I had promised my son that I will be at his game". Sometimes we sacrifice our loved ones simply because we can't set healthy boundaries like saying "I have reserved Saturdays for my kids, so I can't make it".

When you just say "yes" and do something in resentment, you are not doing right by yourself or God himself. A healthy "no" is better before God than a "yes" filled with inner resentment and grumbling.

How to Set and Enforce Healthy Boundaries

It is one thing to know that you should set up boundaries, it is yet another thing to be able to effectively communicate those boundaries in a healthy way. Now that you are aware of the importance of setting boundaries, it is critical that you know how to go about setting them in a healthy way. This is because if setting boundaries is not done in a right way and from the right place and understanding, it won't yield the desired results of inner peace you are hoping to get.

As you set Boundaries, it is critical that you are aware that you are not on a mission to finally tell those people who were crossing the boundaries off. Such an attitude reflects that you are in a bid to revenge and perhaps that your actions are emanating from a negative toxic place. It is important that whatever you do on the journey to emotional health is done from a place of love. If love is not the driving force behind your action, you need to stop, introspect and then put your emotions in order. 1st Corinthians 13 fully explains that some things we do are like noisy bells before God, because they don't come from a place of love. So always examine your intention and emotions and even in a space of having disappointment, ensure that love is the underlying theme.

In setting Boundaries, know that a person who is violating your boundaries might have never known that they were overstepping territory in an unpleasant way towards you. This means that there was never a time when you had communicated these boundaries or expressed reservation about this person's behavior which was resulting in violation of your boundaries. The next major step is communicating those boundaries. How you communicate with them will determine whether you will succeed or fail in setting up the boundary in a healthy way.

When you communicate boundaries, it is important that you employ correct communication skills some of which I will be sharing later on in this book. Timing is important in this process. It is important to have a calm environment in which emotions are under control. Beginning your conversation in a moment where there is no conflict, sets the stage for you to be able to communicate in a kind and loving way without any uncontrollable emotional outbursts. Trying to communicate boundaries when you are emotionally charged, will jeopardize your chances of effective communication. It will not help you drive your point home as it becomes difficult to control your emotions and the words that come out of your mouth when in that state. At this stage you are unable to communicate in a healthy way and this will result in the stripping away of your personal power.

I will demonstrate below a way in which you can express your boundaries in a healthy way.

"Firstly I would like to apologize for letting you assume it was ok to call me after 10pm. I would however like to readdress that and officially inform you that I am not comfortable with receiving calls after 10 pm. If you have an emergency, you could send me a text message, but know that I will not take your calls after 10."

This could be used in any scenario where you start by an apology for not having communicated your boundaries before, allowing them to think it was ok for them to behave in the way they were behaving. After an apology, you then state precisely what your boundary is and the consequence of not adhering to the Boundary.

Expressing your boundaries in a way of love helps for a natural flow in the relationship even after the boundary has been communicated. When a boundary is expressed in this way, even when someone is disappointed in the new boundary, they still know you care for them and they are free to interact in other ways while respecting the boundaries set. Scenarios differ, but this is just a guideline that can help your thought process for boundary communication.

What is important is that you guard your heart, so that you continue to give life and ensure that you are not filled with resentment, toxicity or the need to pretend in relationships. Setting and enforcing personal boundaries will protect your soul and enable you to become emotionally healthy.

DEALING WITH YOUR OWN DYSFUNCTION

What if you are the Toxic One?

As we go through the Journey to Emotional Health, it is all well and good when we discuss our pain, our brokenness and the individuals that have caused us pain. It is easy to unravel how dysfunctional another person is and analyze the potential causes of another's toxic behavior towards you or others. It is however not easy to face the truth in the moment when the light zooms on you, exposing your very own dysfunction and toxicity. Most people tend to shy away from dealing with their own weaknesses but are quick to point out other people's shortcomings. I guess it's human nature. Jesus had this to say about such human attributes in Luke 6:41 *"Why do you see the speck that is in your brother's eye, but do not notice the log that is in your own eye?"*

The truth of the matter is that there is no perfect human on this earth. Time and again we have moments in which we display toxic behavior.

Unknowingly there are times our own dysfunction has lifted up its ugly head in our personalities even when we are unaware. There are these little traits in us that are undesirable and when they go unchecked they have a tendency to negatively impact those we are in relationships with. Journeying to wholeness requires that in as much as we attend to our wounds, we also acknowledge that there are times when we have exhibited behaviors that have wounded others. At times we even believe we are right and justified to continue to behave in a toxic manner. The Bible in the book of Song of Solomon 2:15 thus cautions us this way: *"Catch the foxes for us, the little foxes that spoil the vineyards, for our vineyards are in blossom."* *(ESV)*

It is wise on your journey to emotional health that you pay attention to those little traits (foxes) that spoil the vine, allowing toxicity to flow out of us unknowingly. Emotional Maturity requires that you be bold enough to face your own dysfunction and how it could be negatively impacting others. The goal of this topic is to raise awareness to that side of you that is so easy to ignore and allow you to face it for what it is. I believe this is part of knowing who you are.

For me this realization was awakened by this verse *"Search me, O God, and know my heart: try me, and know my thoughts: And see if there be any wicked way in me, and lead me in the way everlasting."* Psalms 139:23-24 (KJV)
I remember we started praying this verse some time back with a couple of ladies I was praying

with. When we opened ourselves up for that bright light of God to shine on to our weaknesses and wicked ways, the result was far from what we expected. It was hard, it was tough, it was very uncomfortable to see the reality of who we were. I was seeing those negative aspects about myself that God was pointing out. I saw the level of bitterness and unforgiveness I was harboring inside me. I saw how insecure I was and so needy for man's validation. I had always felt comfortable blaming my insecurity on another - declaring that it was someone else's actions that made me insecure. The Lord was pointing out to me that this was my business and I needed to deal with it. This was a very difficult experience. Since then I pray this verse every single day, "Search my heart oh God."

I have become open to allowing God to make me aware of where I'm not behaving right. Sometimes God will have to do extraordinary things in order to make you accept the state of your own dysfunction. Even though we take time analyzing how the dysfunction of others has affected us, this can never change them. As I always say, the only person you have the power to change is you. That is why it is important to face those toxic and negative attributes about you. Not so that they may paralyze you, and cause you to dwell on thoughts like, "Oh no, I'm such a bad person". The mission is to facilitate transformation into a better, healthier version of you. We might never reach perfection, but the goal is to progress and be able to look at your life and say, "I might not have arrived where I'm going, but I am surely not where I used to be", celebrating those little changes and victories as you go along.

The question I am sure everyone is asking now is, "how do I know I am operating from a place of dysfunction?"
I will make a list below of some toxic behaviors that we engage in that negatively affect others we relate to:

- Regular Outbursts of Anger
- Irritability
- Short temperedness
- Bitterness
- Unforgiveness
- Insecurity
- Neediness
- Victimhood
- Passive Aggressive behavior
- Depression
- Sadness
- Looking down on others...

This list is not exhaustive but I'm sure you get the picture

Sad to say that the state of brokenness can create so much dysfunction hence we must be alert of the toxic personality traits that are hidden in our brokenness.

Also be aware that toxic behavior will alienate

you. You will need to assess your behavior to determine if it could be driving people away from you. Indeed, we know there are times when man's rejection has nothing to do with us, but there are times when you need to check yourself when people seem to avoid you. Could it be that your toxic behavior leaves people with no choice but to dissociate with you or love you from afar?

No one wants to nurture a relationship with a grumpy person, a proud person, a mean person, and so on. When you emit negative energy, you drive people away and begin to wonder why people don't want to hang around you. Facing your own dysfunction helps you to know the areas you need to transform and then you can begin working with the Holy Spirit to remove those toxic attributes.

How to Respond to Your Own Dysfunction

This topic may have triggered a level of being unsettled and may have caused you to scrutinize and analyze your own behaviors. It is not my intention that we become caught up in the paralysis of analysis or stuck in feeling horrible and condemned about our dysfunction. The Bible says, "And *you shall know the truth and the truth will set you free*" John 8:32. Engaging with the truth about your own toxicity and dysfunction should be aimed at setting you free and transforming you into a better version of yourself. I would like to share with you some practical tools to help you to deal with your own dysfunction.

1. **Ask God to search your heart.** The first part of my journey began with this prayer: "*Search me, O God, and know my heart: try me, and know my thoughts: And see if there be any wicked way in me, and lead me in the way everlasting.*" Psalms 139:23-24. It is God who knows us well enough to show us the undesirable things in us. He is however, only able to do this if we are committed enough to our betterment that we let him do it. We need to be totally surrendered and ready to hear what he is saying to us. We also need to be willing to change when he points these things out.

2. **Ask God to lead you.** The last part of that verse says "and lead me to the path eternal". It is God who leads. It is God who transforms. Hear me well, you cannot do it on your own. You need the help of the Lord through the Holy Spirit. Thinking you can do it on your own can only lead to paralysis when confronted with failure in trying to change yourself.

Philippians 2:13 "*For it is God who works in you both to will and to do his good pleasure.*" You need the fruits of the spirit from Galatians 5 to be at work in you. The key is to totally depend on the Lord to take you through the journey. "*Trust in the Lord and lean not on your own understanding*" Proverbs 3:5-6.

3. **Know that this is a process,** so you need to be patient with yourself. Changing behaviors that have been part of your life for so long can be a

challenge. Things will not change at the snap of your fingers. Allow for the process of change to happen. The key is to be willing and open to change the behaviors. You also need to allow time for change.

4. **Forgive yourself**. In dealing with your dysfunction and toxic behavior, do not allow condemnation to slip in. Acknowledge that you are only human and a candidate for God's grace and mercy. It is pointless to keep beating yourself down. Perhaps you begin to realize that your actions hurt your kids or spouse and then you start feeling so bad and blaming yourself. Those reactions are counterproductive. Be kind and gracious to yourself knowing what is done, is done. Let it go and focus on changing the future. Godly sorrow should lead to repentance not condemnation. Receive the forgiveness of God and forgive yourself.

5. **Transform**. It is meaningless to have all the light shine on that dysfunction and then continue to stay there. Change and transform your ways. There are some who have normalized their dysfunction. They even pride themselves in it, saying things like "I have a short temper, that's who I am." That is being emotionally immature. Be committed to work for change. If need be, make amends. Actions like apologizing to those you might have hurt are powerful. Once you have apologized, let the apology be followed up with behavioral change. Behavioral change is more meaningful than an apology with no change.

6. **Find Accountability:** As you transform, it is good to have someone you trust to hold you accountable. This helps you stay on track on your journey to transformation. If you need to, get counseling about the issue to enable you to move on.

7. **Seek healing** for wounds that might have caused dysfunction or toxicity. We cannot overemphasize that hurt people hurt others. At times all you need is to get emotional healing and your transformation will come. Be committed to find healing so that pieces from your own brokenness are not cutting onto others.

CHAPTER 8
DEALING WITH EXPECTATION

I'll begin this topic by dropping one of my favorite quotations that I came up with while I was processing my own expectations for people.

"Seek God's approval first before man's approval. Seek God's Love first before man's love. Seek God's provision first before man's provision.... unmet expectations from man, have been a source of much heartbreak and pain, simply because man has limited capacity. God is and has always been the ultimate source for every need you have."

When we speak of 'expectations' we are referring to how in relationships with different people, we have in our minds certain things/ acts we anticipate that they will do for us.

These expectations can be communicated or not communicated to the person who is supposed to render the act. Some of these expectations are just common knowledge, for instance it is a normal expectation for a parent to love and take care of their child. Another commonly agreed on social expectation is that in a marital set up every spouse expects the other spouse to be faithful to them.

They have no need to verbally express this but the day this expectation is not met it will cause untold pain to the expecting individual.

Expectations are normal in relationships, because relationships are all about interaction involving continuous giving and taking by both parties to make a relationship healthy. However, human nature has it that at times people will fail to deliver what is expected of them, simply because they are human. The challenges arise when these unmet expectations bring pain and heartbreak to the person in expectation. Proverbs 13:12 explains it this way: "*Hope deferred makes the heart sick, but a desire fulfilled is a tree of life*". This is exactly what happens as a result of unmet expectations, they make the heart sick.

A situation of the heart being sick creates so much heart ache and misery resulting in a person becoming emotionally unhealthy. In fact, when you take a closer look, most of the pain in relationships is caused by hope deferred or unmet expectations. Wives place expectations on husbands, children place expectations on parents, parents place expectations on their children, pastors, congregants, bosses, employees, presidents, citizens all these groups have expectations on one another.

Becoming emotionally healthy requires an inner understanding of how to deal wisely with unmet expectations, so that your heart continues to be a tree of life even when your expectations are not met. The greatest solution is understanding that humans have shortcomings and can fail to meet your expectations. We should look to the all-knowing, all powerful and all-seeing God as our source for the fulfillment of all our needs. In Psalm 121:1, David demonstrates how to look to God as your ultimate source this way "*I will lift up mine eyes unto the hills, from whence cometh my help. My help comes from the Lord who made heaven and earth*"

When you look to God and make Him your ultimate source, you protect yourself from the pain that comes from deferment of hope, because you have nurtured an understanding that 'EVERY good and perfect gift comes from God'. True that God can cause someone to be an extended arm of his goodness to you, but do not fix your eyes on what you wish for people to do for you. Rather let your expectation be from God. Proverbs 25vs19 warns us that "*Confidence in an unfaithful man in time of trouble is like a broken tooth, and a foot out of joint.*" This simply means that it is risky to put all your hope and confidence in people. When you do that, you are setting yourself up for trouble. For whatever desire you have, let your expectation be from God.

It is important to realize that no human being has the capacity to fulfill all your desires and needs because they are mere man who are also waiting for their needs and desires to be met. You find the Samaritan woman at the well meeting Jesus she was now on the sixth husband, simply because all the other men had failed to fulfill her needs. I love that Jesus said to her 'if you knew who you are talking to, you would ask me for living waters that will never run dry.' We need to embrace Jesus as the ultimate unending source, for whatever it is we may need, be it emotional, material or physical. We must totally rely on Him, the source.

Another interesting case is that of Rachel who was desperately in need for a child, and ended up becoming so upset with Jacob her husband that she said to him '...*Give me children, or else I die*' Genesis 30:1. Unmet expectations can create intense feelings of anger, frustration, bitterness and desperation. The only response Jacob could give was to simply ask her if he was in the place of God to give her this desire. Don't we all do that at times - looking to get from man that which only God can give? There are some of us who are desperately wanting and expecting things from people and this has resulted in us being hurt and frustrated because they have failed or are failing to provide those things.

For instance, the greatest need we have which is love and acceptance, is unconditionally given by the Lord Jesus. The love of Christ is the only love that we are given without condition. Jesus will love you any day even when you are messed up, and even on your best day. The Bible says he loved us before we even loved him. Find true unconditional love in God, know that God did not spare his son simply because he loved us. Some young ladies end up giving away their bodies sexually to guys because they are so desperate to be loved and accepted and when they have done so, they are rejected all the same. At times we are expecting someone to love us, but they simply don't have the capacity to do so. Some people we are expecting to love us are struggling with their own brokenness and in desperate need of love themselves. God is the ultimate love, find love in him and him alone so you can give it to others. You have been accepted by Christ and need not be anything else. Know this "that You are accepted in the beloved" so run with your heart to that place where you are accepted unconditionally.

Other needs that you might expect to be given by others could be joy or happiness. Do not burden people with the responsibility of making you happy. Some are waiting on their spouse to make them happy, not realizing that true Joy is found in God. The Bible says *'The Joy of the Lord is my strength"* Nehemiah 8vs10. Philippians 4:4 emphasizes this again *"Rejoice in the Lord always and again I say rejoice"*

The list of misplaced expectations on people is endless. It can even extend to expectation for finances or provision. In this case, remember Psalm 23:1 *"The LORD is my Shepherd I shall not want"*. God is your provider. Always go to Him with your needs. For others it can be the need for validation, approval or appreciation. People may fail to appreciate the good you are doing for them. Be reminded that God is your exceeding great rewarder, so whatever you do for people, do it as unto the Lord. He will validate and approve you. Let your expectation be from the Lord for everything you need. You will be preserved from much harm and disappointment resulting in an emotionally healthy you.

CHAPTER 9

BECOMING YOUR OWN RESCUE

Taking your personal power back: You are your own Rescue

Let us begin by referring to our previous conversation on expectations which brought us to the understanding that there is always a possibility that people will fall short when it comes to fulfilling our needs. This understanding requires that you shift your expectations from man to God, who has capacity to meet all your needs, be they spiritual, physical, emotional, financial or psychosocial. Operating in such a mind frame helps you become emotionally healthy. It helps you to let go and heal faster from wounds of neglect and unmet expectations from people around you. Forgiveness becomes easier and the quest for your inner peace becomes your responsibility and not anyone else's.

It is from this foundation that you can begin to take full responsibility of everything in your life and stop blaming other people for mishaps in your life. You cannot find wholeness when you are still assigning responsibilities on issues of your life to others. This mental state has helped me to shift my mindset from victimhood, and stop the blame game, allowing me to sit in the drivers' seat of my life and chart the course my life should take through the direction of the Holy Spirit. Such a mindset helps you to take your personal power back. In practice, this means that aspects like my joy, peace and happiness are MY responsibility. God the source of unlimited joy enables me to be joyful in all circumstances. This means I no longer allow another human being to have so much control over my life, that they determine when I am sad or happy.

I am my own rescue and I can do ALL things THROUGH Christ who strengthens me. To become emotionally healthy requires getting rid of this toxic attribute of victimhood in your life. When you arrive at this point you deliberately shift from blaming everyone else for what is wrong in your life, simply because staying in that place is counterproductive and breeds dysfunction in you. We agreed in earlier chapters that it is a given that bad things will happen to us. What really makes us winners in these situations is how we respond to those bad things. We have heard the famous statement that when life gives you lemons, make lemonade out of it. Such a mentality demonstrates to us that our response to any situation, whether good or bad is what will make the difference for a winning life. Even in the worst experiences one can face, your response to the situation is one element you still have control over. You might not be able to control the happenings of a bad event or how other people might treat you badly but you always have a choice on how you will respond. On one end of the spectrum is the option to spend a long time wallowing in your pain and becoming a victim of the situation. This response will create a toxic environment for you and close doors for happiness in your life. You need to find inner strength to rise above situations and transform them for good. Most successful people chose to take charge of their destiny and used their negative experiences as steppingstones to their greatness. It is often in times of great tests in life that extraordinary testimonies come out. This can only happen when you stop being a victim of the situation and begin to take actions that can help you change your situation. Taking responsibility for your life will help you take actions that will bring positive changes.

Some people are stuck in a rut and are sadly waiting for someone to come and rescue them from that place. Some people have assigned responsibility for aspects of their lives to people who don't even know that they carry that responsibility. For instance, some wives are upset that their husbands can't make them happy. These poor men who have been burdened with the role of making sure that their wife is

> *The truth is that the people who hurt you are coming back to heal you, so you need to take responsibility for your own wholeness*

happy are only humans limited in capacity and also trying to find their own happiness as well as battling with their own inner struggles.

The Victimhood Syndrome

'Victimhood Syndrome' can ruin your entire life such that you may never see the door of happiness in your life. A good example of this is Tamar, David's daughter who was raped by her own brother Amnon in a very unfortunate event which took all her pride away. In 2 Samuel 13, the Bible explains that after the incident she poured ashes on herself. Notice that it was not anyone else who put ashes on her, but herself (this is a good example of how we can be our worst enemies at times). The last we hear of her is that she lay 'desolate' in her brother's house. What a sad turn of events, what a sad life! The fact that she had been raped did not change who she was, she was still the daughter of the king, a princess. How many of us have confused our identity with things that, have happened to us? Some of us have even gone to the extent of making our traumas our identity.

After the rape it was Tamar and not anyone else who tore her beautiful coat and poured ashes on herself. This was the response that Tamar chose for herself with regards to her trauma. Your response is far more important than the trauma or hurtful event. I would like to highlight that for every situation that we go through, there are always different options with regard to our response. The secret lies in how we choose to respond. It is critical even in the most terrible situation, be it rejection, failure or loss, that we define ourselves as God sees us, because it is the truth and the truth does not change no matter what happens to us.

When we take full responsibility for our lives, we are able to make choices that lead us to emotional health. We can choose to be happy, no matter the situation. We can decide what we want our future to be. We can choose to wash off the ashes we have put on ourselves and wear our royal robes. We can choose to be healed and whole. We can choose to forgive and live the past behind and work on a better future. We can choose to take action for our prosperity. We have the power within us and, we must never give our personal power away like Tamar did. Notice the recurrence of the word "choose" because you always have a choice with regards your responses to situations.

We can receive beauty 'for' ashes, the garment of praise 'for' the spirit of heaviness, the oil of joy 'for' mourning. Our broken hearts can be bound by Jesus himself. But that choice is yours because for you to receive, you have to give up the ashes to get the beauty. You have to give up the mourning to receive the oil of Joy. You have to give up the heaviness for you to receive the garment of praise. All of these goodies are available to you, but it is up to you to make a decision to pursue inner peace that no one can ever take away from you no matter what situation you find yourself in.

Everything rises and falls on you and the choices you make.

The devil is always lurking behind our traumatic experiences and is always first to present hopelessness in your face. He will work tirelessly to drown you in your sorrows and erase any hope for you to move away from the place in which you are stuck. His entry point is your mind and if you allow him, victimhood will become a full board resident in your mind. Have you noticed that after a traumatic event, self-pity sets into your mind and begins to present all evidence of how disadvantaged you are. As you continue to feed off this state of mind, your emotions are quick to join in the moment creating feelings of sadness. Victimhood is the devil's playground. As you have a pity party, so much negativity fills you up. It is a slippery slope to depression, and all the emotional and physical challenges that come with stress even leading to suicidal thoughts at times. This takes us to one of my quotations on pity parties:

"Don't waste your energy on Pity Parties, the devil himself is the Party Planner, the Host, the MC, the guest of honor, and his guest list is an array of demons straight from hell!! There ain't nothing Holy about a Pity Party!!!!"

Understanding that people will fail you helps you to have peace of mind, trusting God that whatever need you have in any situation, God can actually allow you to receive the solution. You wait on him and not on other people. You cannot allow victimhood to reside in you when you are connected to the source of everything who is God.

"The Rescue Plan" - Building the Inner You To Become Your Own Rescue

At times statements like, 'Becoming Your Own Rescue' can sound like sweeping statements especially when one is feeling trapped and is in a really difficult situation. It may trigger thoughts such as, "You have no idea, you don't know my situation and how much I have had it rough. I have no idea what to do, how can I rescue myself from this situation that I am in? I have tried everything without success.

I will start by sharing a little bit of my story related to this, so that I can give some context in the hope that some will be able to relate. There was a time I felt very overwhelmed with my life, where pretty much most things were not going well. The greatest place that irked me was my marriage. I felt so sad and unhappy, that kind of feeling that this is not what I signed up for. Like most of us, I had unmet expectations. I tried to change my partner to measure up to my expectation. As you can imagine, I failed dismally to my frustration. The day I discovered that there was no person on earth responsible for my joy, was a day of great liberation for me. At this point in my journey I had to really shift focus from blaming someone else and begin to take responsibility for my life. It was not until then that my relationship with my spouse started changing. When I began making personal changes, I noticed that my partner was becoming more and more interested in me and our communication began to improve. Those aspects we discussed in previous chapters on self-love and self-awareness made a big difference for me. A very important lesson I learnt during that time is that 'sometimes the things you are waiting on to change, are waiting for you to change'.

I had been so blind to how my victimhood was so toxic such that it was pushing my husband away. As I made inner changes, I saw him gradually wanting to spend more time with me and creating time for me. There were times I was so grumpy and unhappy that he could not stand being with me. I also realized that I was very insecure and that my neediness and need for validation by him wearied him. It was not easy to accept these negatives about myself, it really rocked my boat. I did realize after this that I was the key to my happiness. Coupled with me changing, I began to decree and declare the things that I felt I wanted and deserved in my marriage on a daily basis. I marvel at the changes that came when I began to change. My environment will respond to what is happening in me and I have the power to facilitate that change.

At times we are our greatest enemies through resigning and throwing in the towel with regards to becoming our own rescue.

I would like you to consider areas in your life that are really worrying you. Be it your marriage or relationship with someone, your finances, your job, your weight and choose to take charge and to be responsible for your own affairs. I am aware that people will treat you unfairly and do mean things such that you may have apportioned the blame for where you are today on people and situations. It could be` experiences such as rejection and abandonment from childhood and for some it could be a series of events that have left you disadvantaged. Whatever the source is, don't underestimate the power you have to change your environment. What is needed is that you take your personal power back and don't leave your life to fate.

Even though it could be the result of another person's mean actions that you find yourself in the difficulty you are in today, it is still your 'RESPONSIBILITY' to take your life where you would like it to be. Understanding that whatever people do is not a reflection of who you are but a reflection of who they are and how they see themselves will help you not to take things people do too personally. The key is to snap out of being stuck in apportioning the blame to people and events and to rise above all this and become your own rescue.

Steps to Becoming Your Own Rescue
1. The first step is shifting your mindset from placing expectations on people and shifting them to God being the immediate (very present) and ultimate helper. Always lift your eyes to God instead of putting your expectation on what people can do for you. I like how David the Psalmist explains situations of extreme turmoil and how God is the very present help in Psalm 46. He talks about a river that is in the midst of the city of God, and that He will help her early. He even goes on to say," be still and know that I am God". David explains it further in Psalm121:1-2 "*I will lift up mine eyes to the hills, from whence cometh my help. My help comes from the Lord which made heaven and earth.*" Looking to God as our immediate help shields us from the disappointment and pain of un-met expectation. When your eyes look to God as the ultimate source you have no need to blame anyone for your situation and you are setting yourself up for a definite win in every situation.

2. Having the awareness that God has already put in you all the resources you need to make it. 2 Peter 1:3 says that "*As His divine power has given to us all things that pertain to life and godliness, through the knowledge of him who called us by glory and virtue.*" Everything that we need has already been given to us, meaning there is nothing we need to achieve and get in this life

that we cannot get. Situations and challenges we go through in life can cause us to doubt this, but we always need to remind ourselves that we are adequate and enough for what life throws at us. Also knowing that our God ordained purpose was set before we were even conceived as Jeremiah describes, *"Before I formed thee in the belly, I knew thee: and before thou camest forth out of the womb I sanctified thee and ordained thee prophet to the nations."* Jeremiah 1:5

3. Change your perspective, there is always another side of the story to what you are facing. Ephesians 4:23 *"And be renewed in the spirit of your mind."* It is critical to be aware of the perspective you have about any situation. Most challenges that you are facing in your life right now are all about perspective and the story you tell yourself about the situation. Two people can be in the very same situation but what makes the difference is how they view their situation. I love how the prophet Zechariah puts it in Zechariah 4:7. *"Who art thou, O great mountain before Zerubbabel, thou shall become a plain."* This was a winning mindset, the mountain situation was there, but the attitude was that he would conquer.

4. When you change your mindset it is now time to speak the change into your life. Amidst discouraging reports from their Israelite company, Caleb and Joshua simply stated **"We are well able."** You can choose to make a

declaration that you are well able to rise no matter how bad the situation looks. Proverbs 18:20 says *"Death and life are in the power of the tongue and they that love it shall eat the fruit thereof"*. The things that we say during our difficult times are a lifeline which will determine whether we will make it or not. Most people who set up residence in victimhood have consistently allowed self-defeating words to come out of their mouths. We need to realize that we have so much power in the words of our mouth to change the course of our future and we should use this power wisely through positive declarations. Make a conscious decision every single day as you wake up, to rescue yourself by speaking and declaring for change. I have dubbed it 'a daily rescue mission'. Do not be silent, speak to it positively speak the word and you will see it yielding. This is a critical step in becoming your own rescue.

5. Take action for the changes you want to see. Some have become so helpless in their situations and feel that they cannot do anything about where they are. This is a lie of the devil that wants to keep you stuck in that place. The truth is that there is always something you can do about your situation. I am always reminded about the four lepers mentioned in 2 Kings 7:3-4 *"And there were four leprous men at the entering in the gate: and they said one to another, why stay we here and die? 4 If we say, we will enter into the city, then the famine is in the city, and we shall die there: and if we sit*

still here, we shall die also. Now therefore come, and let us fall into the host of the Syrians: If they save us alive, we shall live, and if they kill us we shall but die"

How many times have we found ourselves in situations so bad and helpless that doing anything seems risky? The lepers here realized that becoming victims and just sitting there was no solution. It is exciting to see how God made a way for them through a great deliverance in the Syrian camp. Taking action, no matter how small or insignificant is key to moving from the place of victimhood. When you take one small action it makes room for more action. I have seen that God honors the small steps we take and He always steps in to amplify them. Even when the Israelites were standing in front of the Red Sea crying out to God, his instruction to them was to stop crying and move forward. God always comes through in ways we could have never imagined when we take bold steps. God works with us to become our own rescue when we begin to take action from our places of victimhood.

For instance, if your issue is getting out of poverty to a place of financial freedom, start thinking of ways you can begin right where you are. Perhaps all you have is a gift to plait hair, that is a project you can do without any capital. At times it might mean just planting vegetables in your garden and begin selling. Some people are waiting for something big and miraculous to happen, yet the miracle begins with you. Some people feel ashamed to do things that they might feel are humiliating for their status. When you are still thinking like that you haven't been irked by your situation enough. You have to do whatever it takes irrespective of what people may say or think about you. It is your life and your responsibility and at times it might mean doing a job lower than your status, do whatever it takes. I remember l having to go to places where people wouldn't usually see me for my peanut butter project. I did what I had to do, to become my own rescue. As you take action remember never to give up, even in the face of failure keep moving and keep on trying there is success waiting for you right ahead.

What is My "Why"? - Eliminating Excuses

Oftentimes in situations of victimhood, people have excuses and explanations for why it is so difficult to come out of the place they are in. Your explanations are filled with **'why'** you can't do this or that. To rescue yourself out of a rut you may be in, you will need to evaluate your reasons and excuses for having stayed there in the first place. Facing your excuses and seeing them for what they really are will help you come up with strategic interventions to eliminate those excuses. For you to be able to become your own rescue you need to practice introspection and ask important questions. The question to ask yourself is this **"What is my why?"** What is it that you are waiting for?

In answering these critical questions, you begin to remove barriers, limitations, and excuses you have held on to for a long time. These barriers and excuses always make you feel like you are helpless and have no way out. The victim state puts all the responsibility for your survival and improvement in the hands of those you think can help. One big challenge I've come across is that when someone is in a state of victimhood, they tend to see themselves as a charity case, waiting for someone to come and rescue them.

A friend shared with me an audio of a Zimbabwean motivational speaker, Arthur Marara. He made a very powerful statement about becoming your own rescue which has stuck to me until today. This statement is **"NO ONE IS COMING!!"** You need to live your life knowing that NO ONE IS COMING to rescue you. If you do not take initiative to change the way things are in your life you will be stuck for life. Everyone is occupied and so busy with their own lives, so know that and adjust accordingly.

Reason and Excuse

I want you to catch these two words **REASON** and **EXCUSE**. For an example there is a reason you are in the situation you are in today. Reasons are the negative things that have brought you to the place you are in today. Reasons will always vary depending on the situation. Some examples of reasons are a disadvantaged background, your childhood, rejection, bereavement, or even your bad decisions. These scenarios described here constitute the reason you are in that state. The challenge now comes when a person begins to use the REASON as an EXCUSE not to move forward. For instance, the reason a widow might find herself struggling to go on would be that she lost her husband who was the breadwinner. Someone operating from the victim mentality will spend years in mourning, helplessly waiting for others to help. Another widow will realize that it is her responsibility to rise up and take care of the family while the "victim widow" continues to spend years using her REASON as an EXCUSE. This is why you see amazing stories of people who were born without hands learning to write and do extraordinary things. These kind of people make a choice not to make their reason an excuse.

Exercise on "Being You Own Rescue"

1. Take a piece of paper and in the middle of that paper draw a circle where you will write your name.

2. Around the center put these titles in squares: *Spiritual, Marriage, Family, Career/ Work. Finances, Purpose, Education and any area that is specific to you*

3. Around these sub topics write your wish list like

what your dreams are for these areas. Eg in marriage you can write, happiness, peace, oneness - Where you wish to be, your ideal representation for each area.

4. After this wish list go to each wish and answer this question - "What can I do to achieve this?" Sometimes it is coming up with one simple action. Maybe on Education you may have a wish to get a degree, the first step would be, to apply for a place at a University. I am hoping this exercise will trigger small actions in the right direction to change your life through becoming responsible for the change you want to see.

CHAPTER 10

WINNING COMMUNICATION FOR EMOTIONAL HEALTH

Have you ever said one thing only to discover that what you have been trying to communicate has been totally misunderstood and has in fact been taken to negative levels you never intended at all? In such moments you end up being dumbfounded and failing to comprehend how what you meant to say even got there? Unhealthy communication can take a negative toll on your emotions, leaving you at times hurt and confused. James 3:5 says this *"Even so the tongue is a little member, and boasteth great things. Behold, how great a matter a little fire kindleth!"*

Good communication is key to successful relationships and the quality of your communication can either deplete your state of emotional health or increase it. Intelligent and powerful communication has a way of strengthening you and building your inner resilience empowering you to achieve a healthy state in your mind and emotions. Great communication skills create good understanding and intimacy between you and those close to you. This is one area I continue building muscle for daily as I have started seeing and experiencing the benefits of good communication. In my journey I realized that the ability to communicate my needs and issues enabled me to sustain my personal power and also be listened to and be respected in relationships. In the past I used to be such an emotional wreck who failed dismally in communicating my issues especially to my spouse. This destroyed my self-esteem as conversations would not end well, leaving me hurt and helpless at the same time. In my experience, bad communication has the ability to take your greatly needed personal power away. if we become more conscious of the ways in which we communicate we can improve and become more effective communicators. These are the tools I would like to share in this chapter.

The word of God is awash with scriptures on the impact of communication and how much power communication wields. Our point of departure and reference is what the word says about communication.

"Let your speech be always with grace, seasoned with salt, that ye may know how ye ought to answer every man." Colossians4:6-7

"Let no corrupt communication proceed out of your mouth, but that which is good to the use of edifying, that it may minister grace unto the hearers." Ephesians 4:29 KJV

"Wherefore, my beloved brethren, let every man be swift

*to hear, slow to speak, slow to wrath: For the wrath of
man worketh not the righteousness of God."* James
1:19-20 KJV

*"There is one whose rash words are like sword thrusts,
but the tongue of the wise brings healing."* Proverbs
12:18

*"Instead, speaking the truth in love, we will grow to
become in every respect the mature body of him who is
the head, that is, Christ "*Ephesians 4:1

In this chapter I will share practical tips for
winning communication. I will describe scenarios
and share effective communication strategies that
can help us to become better communicators.

Practical Communication Scenarios and Strategies.

**Strategy 1: When faced with a difficult or
sensitive issue that you need to discuss with
someone close such as spouse, parent, sibling or
close friend:**
In scenarios where you need to discuss a difficult
or sensitive issue with someone close to you, it is
critical that you are emotionally prepared because
such scenarios can easily spiral into serious
disagreements or arguments. One must therefore
be self-aware and totally present to avoid any
mishaps during communication.

- As you begin to communicate your issue, come
  from a stand-point of love while speaking the

truth in love.

- It is important to highlight that you are on the same team with the individual and that you respect and love him/ her.
- Always be careful that you are not emotional when you speak, as it is easy to lose self-control when emotions begin to fly all over the place.
- Do not ramble as you communicate, be precise and brief, clearly stating your issues.
- Be sure not to make accusations against the other person as this can cause them to become defensive, rather state how the issue affects you or makes you feel.
- Do not present your issue when you are in a state of anger, take some time to cool off and then come when you are emotionally ready for discussion and not a confrontation.

For example, in a scenario where a wife is unhappy about the way her husband spoke to her, she would craft her conversation in this manner. *"Honey I want you to know that I love and respect you. Always remember that we are on the same team. I wanted you to know that earlier on I was not happy with the way you spoke to me. It made me feel unloved and uncared for and really hurt me"*

Notice the use of the word 'feel" rather than statements like "You don't love me, or you don't care for me". The focus here is now more on how the event made her feel a certain way. The latter can easily come across as an accusation which can lead to your significant other becoming defensive and emotional during the conversations. When someone feels that they are being accused in a conversation, it can feel like an attack which triggers an immediate response to defend themselves. This doesn't enable healthy conversation. Focusing instead, on how something made you feel, moves the conversation from them and draws them to be more empathic to your feelings. Other things to pay attention to in such a conversation are as follows:

- Do not globalize issues by using statements like, "You ALWAYS do ...." "EVERYTIME you ...." This diverts the conversation from the issue at hand and can stir up strife in the conversation, making it counterproductive in communication.

- Stick to the issue at hand and don't start presenting your file of record of wrong with all the things you were bottling inside.

- Freely express how you wish things could happen next time in a similar scenario. eg "*I would appreciate it in future if you could raise such issues in the absence of the kids*"

- This is also a wise time to express any boundaries that you might feel have been violated.

- The issue of timing is very important when discussing a difficult or sensitive issue. Know the right time to bring your issues up. Wrong timing will mess it up for you. it is wise to raise your issue in a moment when both of you are high spirited and calm. Try not to bring up a sensitive issue when either of you is still angry so that your emotions are controlled during the conversation.

- Be aware and prepared for the possibility that the conversation might not go well or might not be well received by the other especially if it is already a sensitive issue. If at any point you see the discussion getting out of hand, keep quiet or excuse yourself from discussion respectfully and promise to revisit it in a state of calmness. Don't allow yourself to be sucked into an argument. This takes serious inner strength as it is easier said than done.

- Keep it short and to the point. Do not get emotional because it can spiral into something else resulting in loss of self-control. In this state, it is easy to lose the reigns and end up saying things you didn't mean to say.

Strategy 2: "Communication Strategies in a Fierce Conflict"

Proverbs 13:3 "*He that keepeth his mouth keepeth his life: but he that openeth wide his lips shall have destruction*"

Conflict is part of a normal relationship, and it is more likely to occur and be more intense, the closer you are to a person. This is because all of us are different and we have different views about issues. Unmet expectations can spiral into conflict when they are pointed out by one of the parties. I have noticed that the things that worry us in relationships can become repeated conflict especially when there is failure to come to a peaceful resolution regarding the issue. Unresolved conflicts can really strain the relationship and weigh both of the parties down. They can also invoke negative feelings like anger, pain, hurt, betrayal or mistrust to the extent that we have heard of extreme cases where people end up getting physically violent, shooting or stabbing the other, leading to loss of life. The big component in conflict is communication and a failure to communicate an issue effectively can ruin relationships. The ability to navigate conflict in a healthy way is key for a successful relationship.

Proverbs 15: 1 says this *"A gentle answer turns away wrath, but a harsh word stirs up anger"*

I remember a point in my life when I struggled to deal with conflict. While in a heated argument I would feel something rising from my belly, while tapping my feet on the ground hoping I could stop that thing from erupting. As I continued in the conflict, I would feel this thing rising until it reaches the top of my head. It would then just erupt like a fizzy bottle of Coca-Cola that had been shaken. When I reached that stage, all hell would break loose and there would be no telling, the things that would come out of my mouth at that point. I know there are some who can relate to this experience. This reflected that during that time I had not built enough skill to handle moments of fierce conflict in a healthy way. As I committed myself to pursuing personal growth and partnered with the Holy Spirit, I began building on my communication skills. I continue to work on improving the way I handle moments of conflict, but I have definitely come a long way since then.

Equipping oneself with winning communication strategies and relying on the Holy Spirit can help one maintain self-control and keep a potentially explosive conflict under control. The challenge with most of these conflicts are that you are never prepared for them, they can just begin even when you least expect them. The moment you see disagreement creating tension, it is important that you put your guard up and notice the progression and direction of the discussion. There is a point when trying to make your point that you become aware that your internal alarms have been triggered and, you will need to decide whether to proceed or not.

1. The first thing you need to do, is to get hold of your emotions and calm down. If you see yourself having to raise your voice to make a point you will need to lower your voice and speak calmly. A gentle answer turns away wrath. This is actually

God's promise. Trust God that when you put it into effect it will work for you.

2. However if you see that things seem to be getting out of hand, even with your soft answer or that you are now finding it difficult to give the soft answer, this is your cue to withdraw from the argument for the sake of peace. You can do this by either just not responding to the person or allow them to win the argument. The usual statement I just say is *"ok I see "*or *"I hear you"* and then not get sucked into the argument. If you see them wanting to continue with the argument and suck you in further, you can simply say something like *"I think I cannot continue with this discussion right now, I will go and do the laundry, or take a walk* (whatever you want to do). *We can continue the discussion later when we are both calm."*

Say this with absolute respect so that it is well received and never forget to do it from the place of love. Always be aware not to say too many words, keep it short and walk away or just keep quiet if you are unable to move away from the place you are. Don't allow your emotions to give in, as that can result in you saying a whole lot of things that can hurt the other. Try to ensure that you are not out of control thereby giving your personal power away. Things said can never be erased and in moments of uncontrolled emotions it's easy to say things that can hurt others.

3. The other person may continue to speak and be out of control to the extent that they start hurling

insults and false accusations at you. They may say things like, 'you are stubborn, you are selfish, you are foolish, you don't care about me, ... etc.'. The first instinct is to try to defend yourself when accusations are presented to you. The most likely reaction is to say, "no, I am not like that" or "I never said or did that." The moment you get into defense mode, you are getting drawn back into the conflict. In as much as you will have this urge to defend yourself in this moment, do not do so. It is a perfect time to remember your authentic identity and that you are not who they say you are. Do not receive their insults by placing an emotional blocker against these nasty words. In that scenario, just keep quiet and leave them to it. If you feel you want to respond, you can simply say short precise statements like "I am sorry you see things that way." Know in your heart that they are entitled to their own opinion and you don't have to receive it. Leave it there and say no more. In your mind, resist negative demeaning things said to you by others.

4. Another tactic you can use in that scenario to keep yourself grounded and prevent your emotions from going haywire, is to visualize yourself grounded and in control of your emotions. In that moment, imagine that you have roots going down from your feet into the ground emotionally. Ensuring that you are grounded in your mind will help you to be resilient enough enabling you to remain in control of your emotions.

5. Another way that will help minimize the impact

of false accusations and negative words is to imagine yourself enclosed by a glass wall and that you cannot hear what they are saying. Create that wall in your mind so that your soul does not receive these insults. There is a time I used to say, "back to sender" in my heart. I then realized that was not from the place of love hence I now just visualize that glass wall blocking the negative energy from entering my soul.

6. After you walk away from the conflict and you've managed to suppress your emotions, find a safe space you can go to, whether it's the bathroom, another room, the car or taking a walk etc. In this space allow yourself to process the emotions. If you need to shed a tear, to scream or just shout back, do it in that space. What is important is that you don't bottle up the emotions, but find a way of releasing them in a safe place. After having controlled your emotions remember that all that negative energy from the fierce conflict needs an outlet otherwise it will linger around in your space causing pain and creating wounds. Process the experience by finding a safe place to vent and let it out. Tell the Holy Spirit how you truly feel in that moment and allow him to comfort you and heal you if need be.

7. Always reach out to the Holy Spirit for help, to empower you to grow in the fruits of the spirit and self-control. Allow him to be your partner at all times to help you respond in moments of conflict. Allow feelings of peace to flood your heart, and the Holy Spirit to make you the peace

maker. Blessed are the peacemakers for they shall be called the children of God. The only person you can change is you. As you change for peace and become a peace maker, conflicts will be easily diffused.

Responding vs Reacting In Fierce Conflict

This strategy is a more or less a continuation of the strategy we have just discussed above on handling fierce conflict. We look closer at 'responding' vs 'reacting' and how best you can control your mind and emotions.

Have you ever been in a conversation and you say something, only to realize that what the other person is thinking you said is actually not what you said? That whole conversation can go out of context to an extent that you will not remember what the discussion was about. When misunderstood, the first instinct is to react and when you react there is a high likelihood that you will lose the direction you had hoped for the discussion to take.

The art of learning to respond vs reacting in a potentially explosive interaction is one that will help you maintain your personal power and enable you to have healthy conversations with others. We are made with the stimulus to react when we feel a threat coming our way. The challenge that comes with reacting is that, usually you are not in control of your reactions during conflict. Most reactions are driven by a force emanating from a place of emotional pain and hurt.

This means that reactions do not provide a sound place to sustain your personal power as your reactions can potentially go all over the place because they are driven by emotion. This is counterproductive when trying to have healthy conversations especially when there are disagreements. It is important to learn to respond rather than react in times of conflict. Learning to respond is more difficult than reacting as it requires mastery and strength of character which we aim to build up in you through this journey.

The first thing you need to be aware of in any given scenario, is that your response to any situation is your responsibility. Take note of the two words in the word responsibility 'response and ability'. In other words, responsibility is your ability to respond. What the other person says to you whether to provoke you or to hurt you is their responsibility, but how you respond is always your responsibility no matter how bad the situation is or what has been said to you.

Responding, unlike reacting, requires that you take a moment to think about how you respond. The big question then is 'how do you do this in the moment of conflict?' I always remember myself in some scenarios where I would be falsely accused or insulted during conversations. I would have a thousand things to say to this person in my mind. That one hurtful thing that I had been waiting to say to him/ her for a long time or the negative thoughts that had been lingering in my mind about this person would come screaming in my mind to be said in that moment. All those are reactionary words and trust me when said, produce no good. Remember in the previous lesson we mentioned that we have a choice to become the peace makers in the time of conflict. So it is critical that when thoughts come to your head, you begin to sift through for thoughts that create a peaceful atmosphere.

To help you do this in the moment of conflict, remember the skills we learnt so far, but add the following skills as well to keep you more in control of your mind, your mouth and your emotions.

1. Firstly before any word comes out of your mouth, take a deep breath, you can even extent them to three deep breaths. This allows you time to calm your emotions down and to sift through your thoughts for a response. I started doing this exercise with my kids when they are in distress, only to realize this was also very good for me. It helps you also to take charge of yourself and center yourself. Taking deep breaths reaches out for the real you and help you to take control of emotions like anger or just lashing out in the moment. Do not be in a rush at any time to speak. A support scripture to this skill is James 1: 19 *"My dear brothers and sisters, take note of this: Everyone should be quick to listen, slow to speak and slow to become angry"*

2. As you are in this breathing phase, take note of your thoughts. The Bible says, "from the abundance of the heart the mouth speaks." Try to go to that place of love in your heart where you can scan for responses. This is not always easy in heated scenarios but when you become slower at responding, it can be done. Remind yourself of such scriptures which you can also be declaring every day of your life so that they don't just appear when you are in a reactionary phase or conflict. Proverbs 31: 26 *"She openeth her mouth with wisdom; and in her tongue is the law of kindness"* Kindness is a law and you can train your mouth in kindness even in the most difficult environment. Always remember that the law of kindness is not weakness, it is strength as you trust in God and not in your own ability to fight for yourself in different scenarios. The law of kindness comes from the place of love and 'love never fails'

3. Ask yourself this question 'do you want to be right or do you want to be happy?' At times being right comes at the cost of fueling a potentially fierce conflict where both of you begin to raise voices and become emotional in trying to prove your point. When the conflict continues in this way with both parties trying to prove their points, it will be difficult to end the conflict as no one is willing to lose the argument or to not have the last word. This can stir up the conflict resulting in a lot of negativity like anger, hurt, pain or sadness. To avoid these negatives, it's critical that you choose your desired result. There are times you fight to be right and risk losing peace and joy in

that moment or for a longer period than you had anticipated. In responding, choose your desired end and be willing to face the consequences.

I am aware that this way of thinking can be criticized by others because some people believe for you to be happy, you always have to stand up for yourself and prove your point otherwise you become a door mat or pushover while people do what they want with you. I agree that standing up for yourself is right, but when it results in you losing control of your emotions, there is no winning there. Note that there are healthier ways to stand up for yourself that don't require you to lose your emotions. That is what you need to skill yourself in, going back to how to set healthy boundaries. One thing you will realize is that it takes more strength of character and restraint to walk away in a conflict than to stand there and prove your point. Knowing when to leave or back down in a conflict for the sake of peace has a way of disarming the other party because now he/ she has no reason to proceed in the conflict.

Lastly, when you choose to take the high road of responding versus reacting, always remember that you can succumb to insults and false accusations. Keep your emotions in balance, avoid reacting to these insults or trying to defend yourself like we mentioned earlier. Rather give calm short responses like, "I am sorry you feel that way" or "I see." If you choose to leave the discussion, excuse yourself calmly from continuing in the argument. If you choose to keep quiet and not respond, be watchful of your NON- VERBAL communication. It should not be emotional in anyway, just stay cool and show no agitation. Don't do things like storming out or throwing your hands in the air or show emotions like anger or sadness on your face as this is also part of reacting. Such reactions can be viewed by another as passive aggressive behavior, so remember to do everything from the place of love and then later process the emotions in a safe place.

Passive Aggressive Behavior (PAB)

Passive Aggressive behavior is a form of non-verbal communication which involves the use of silent protests such as silent treatment, sulking, refusal to eat, withholding affection or financial support to another. It can also manifest in outright intentional bypassing or ignoring another individual as a way of emotionally torturing the recipient of PAB. A person exhibiting this behavior will use passive aggressive actions rather than communicating their dissatisfaction with words. This is the worst form of communication and can cause emotional torture to the person on the receiving end as they are unable to receive any form of verbal communication as to why someone is behaving in this way. Some people use this form of communication to punish a person for having offended them in a certain way. Others do it from a place of their own dysfunction and inability to communicate in a healthy way.

PAB is not good because one has not verbalized

what they are trying to communicate during their display of PAB. The interpretation of their actions lies in the receiver. When a person exhibits this behavior, they stand to be misunderstood and such behavior can potentially grow into something that was never intended due to misunderstanding of what is being communicated by the behavior. PAB can be destructive and potentially damage relationships when it is frequently done or continues on for long periods.

Trying to communicate one's grievances using PAB is not beneficial because the other party might not be clear as to what is being communicated through your actions. The result is that it might not yield the expected response or behavioral change in the person you are addressing it to. Another issue with regards to PAB is that the person is operating from a place where emotions are in control of their actions. Emotional reactions often give personal power away for instance when someone sulks and refuses to eat the meal that has been placed in front of them just to prove that they are angry at someone. It will be difficult to reverse the actions when they are no longer angry and realize that they are hungry and need a meal. They might be forced to go long periods in hunger due to the shame of their protest.

This behavior can also result in more suffering for the person engaging in it while trying to sustain the protest. Imagine when one is in a bad mood and giving a spouse the silent treatment and your spouse continues to have a good time with the kids and laughing while you have declared you are not talking to him/her. When they start having a good time or laughing and you are in your self-made prison you won't be able to join in even if you really want to share that good time with them. What a miserable state to be in. I know people who can sustain these habits for long periods like 3 weeks or more. This is not good as it opens you up to a lot of negative feelings and thoughts and can allow your mind to be the devil's workshop. It takes a lot of negative resolve to sustain PAB. To sustain this behavior for long periods a person has to feed into this negativity with thoughts of hate, bitterness and anger. While you think you are punishing the other party, you tend to punish yourself more in the process. This is an unhealthy way of resolving issues and does not enhance your emotional health.

PAB vs Anger Outbursts

I am aware that for some it is simpler to slip into PAB just to avoid saying things in anger. Due to various factors there are some who prefer to take this route. When someone lashes out in anger, there is a high chance of saying things they could regret for life. The key is to develop these communication skills, take time to process your feelings when you are alone and then presenting your issue in a mature manner while expressing your concern in a way that ensures you will be heard.

I was however on the other end where I found it hard to contain my feelings and I would recklessly burst out, this never helped but left me hurt and at times in a worse state than before.

Passive aggressive behavior (PAB) on the other hand also does great harm. Bottling your feelings and then protesting with (PAB) has the inner mission of punishing the person who hurt you. The downside it has is that you have to sustain elongated periods of anger and extreme negative emotions. The Bible instructs this way *''Be ye angry and sin not: let not the sun go down on your anger, Neither give place to the devil"* Ephesians 4: 26-27. The reason God gives this instruction is because anger broods extreme negatives if incubated for long periods. I will give an example - let's say there is trash in a bin, as time progresses in the right atmosphere, the trash begins to rot, stink and eventually those gruesome worms start coming out. That is what anger does when it is incubated in your heart. Ecclesiastes 7:9 *"says Do not be quickly provoked in your spirit, for anger resides in the lap of fools"*. Long periods in a state of PAB allows your mind to meditate on how much a person has wronged you and fills your heart with so much negativity and rot - thoughts of bitterness, revenge, wishing evil for that person who hurt you, hatred, insults and all negatives you can imagine. Such a soul becomes the Devil's workshop and makes you emotionally unhealthy. it is important to develop better conflict resolution strategies and nurture your soul to be full of love and joyful at all times.

This is healthy for you both emotionally and physically.

Extreme Passive Aggressive Behavior

We have already discussed how PAB can be taken to extreme levels in some cases by people with extreme emotional disorders or are emotionally unhealthy. These extreme levels of PAB can become emotionally abusive as they are meant to exert a level of torture on the victim. People who engage in this type of behaviour, are very damaged inside. They are looking for ways to reassert their identity and authority. Taking a closer look at their past experiences you would learn that they were wounded at some stages maybe while growing up. They may have experienced some level of abuse or unbalanced parenting in which they got everything they wanted. These people aim to control people close to them with silent treatment, aggression or deprivation of things others need like love, intimacy, or emotional and financial support. When it gets to such extreme measures, it is important to pay attention to what is happening for the sake of your emotional health.

Strategies on How to Respond To PAB

A key is for the receiver of PAB, is to be whole and emotionally healthy to help them handle the stress of experiencing it and making sure they sustain joy in a hostile environment. Make sure you fill your heart and mind with the right thoughts and don't allow how another person is treating you to define who you are. Find love in God and focus your mind on positive thoughts. Do not allow yourself to be enslaved in unhappiness because of someone else's behavior. Another person's behavior is not your responsibility so don't feed their need for control.

However, elongated periods receiving PAB is not good and healthy, neither is it God's plan for your life. When a person engages in this behavior, know that they are operating in another realm and you will need to engage in spiritual warfare. Talking to such a person about their behavior might not necessarily change them, but talking to God about it and praying for them is important. *"The weapons of our warfare are not carnal but mighty through God to the pulling down of strongholds"*. You will need to find appropriate scripture to take your battle to the spirit level. Finding support could also help in coping with this behavior.

Dealing with False Accusation

Being in a conflict where you feel like you are being falsely accused can be a very difficult place to be, as the urge to prove your innocence can cause you to be extremely emotional. We know now that reacting in an emotional way will not yield a positive atmosphere for you. When faced with an accuser and he/she feels they are right, arguing with them to prove yourself right will drain energy from you. The best stance is to let them be. You don't necessarily have to apologize for the sake of peace especially when you know you are not what they are saying you are. Alternative peaceful words you can say are, "I'm sorry you feel that way" thereby you are not accepting the accusation but you are showing empathy towards how they are feeling. In your heart do not receive the accusations, just keep quiet. Saying "Sorry" just so that the issue goes away is not a healthy way to resolve the conflict, simply because it is based in falsehood and not coming from a place of authenticity. In such scenarios, I encourage you to listen and not respond.

At times, the person accusing you can escalate things through manipulative statements or hurling insults at you. That is the moment you know that your accuser has a bigger agenda than what you are seeing. These go back to that person looking for control over you and your emotions. An effective strategy is not to fight back, just reduce your words, yield yourself, and go with the flow. Observe and listen but place that invisible glass door in your mind so that you do not receive what they are saying. Continue to nurture yourself while reminding yourself who God says you are and declare positive things about you and your relationship with this person.

The truth is that it is not always easy. You need a lot of grace and help from the Holy Spirit as you mature more and more and become whole. In the times you fail to communicate effectively, do not beat yourself up. Always be quick to forgive yourself and let it go. These situations can indeed be intense and continuing to reach out to the Holy Spirit for help and comfort is necessary.

"Praise be the God and Father or our Lord Jesus Christ, the Father of compassion and the God of all comfort, who comforts us in all our troubles, so that we can comfort those in any trouble with the comfort we ourselves receive from God." 2 Corinthians 1:3

Becoming the Peacemaker

You can CHOOSE to be the peace in the conflict or be the conflict itself. Conflicts will confront us so often but when you have received the peace of God in your heart and are committed to a peaceful environment, even that argumentative urge in you starts to disappear. Understanding also that on your part quarrels are an indication of unhealthy emotional patterns within you. James 4:1 (NET) says this *"Where do the conflicts and where do the quarrels among you come from? Is it not from this, from your passions that battle inside you"*

Peace begins with you and God can make you the channel of peace in your home or anywhere it is needed. But you have to be committed to being a peace maker. When you shine light into a space, darkness just disappears. Peace is a light you can decree and shine into your space on a daily basis.

I remember a season in my life where almost every discussion with my spouse would end up in conflict. In those moments I would fail to control my emotions and would raise my voice trying to defend myself or ensure my point was heard.

There came a point when I decided that I wanted peace. I looked up scriptures on peace, touched the walls of my home declaring peace. These communication skills came later but as I began to choose the way of peace, and trusting God enough to fight for me, He would vindicate me when I needed him to. When you have peace within you can trust God with your battles so that He fights on your behalf.

As I became the peace maker, I slowly began to see that change beginning with me. Always be aware that you connect with people at the level of your emotional state whether wholeness or brokenness. You can never fake your inner state, meaning that time and again you will project what is going on inside you involuntarily. When you continuously quarrel, it is a reflection of what is happening inside you. That is why wholeness and being emotionally healthy will create a powerful foundation for winning communication.

Arguments can be so draining, to an extent that exhaustion can be seen on your face, in your mind and body. This is altogether unhealthy, emotionally, physically and spiritually so learning these winning communication strategies is important for your overall wellbeing. Also be aware that the devil is at work and does not want harmony and peace so always be spiritually alert and conscious when the 3rd man (Satan) invades your space through your conversations with others. That is when you realize that allowing yourself to be drawn into these arguments at times gives the 3rd man material to work with. The times when you choose not to be drawn into moments of conflict will disarm the devil.

When we start learning things, you will realize that tests will come, like now that you have learnt about these winning communication strategies, do not be surprised if you start encountering more and more opportunities to practice these skills. When you become more self-aware and self-loving, those around you may not be understanding the changes and what is happening to you, but as long as you continue to be true to yourself and operate from the place of love, you will not fail, because love never fails. Strive to be the best version of yourself as you immerse yourself in positive thoughts and feelings. Continue to see yourself the way God sees you, and never stop speaking it into being because you can change your situation through the words of your mouth. Allow God to touch and heal your wounds so that wholeness becomes your portion. Strive for peace in your heart, hope and love for yourself and others.

CHAPTER 11

AN ATTITUDE OF GRATITUDE

An attitude of gratitude is a critical element in living an emotionally healthy life. The biggest enemy to gratitude is the need to grumble and complain about how badly you have had it in life. This kind of attitude breeds a toxic atmosphere of negativity, nursing bitterness, hurt, and pain. That having been said, it's easy to be grateful when everything seems to be in order and you are experiencing breakthrough after breakthrough. It however becomes a different story when you have to give thanks in the face of trouble, hurts, trials and difficult times. Trials have a way of diverting attention from the areas in your life that are in order.

As I compiled this lesson on thanksgiving, God had to allow this lesson to be real in my life perhaps so that I would be able articulate it from experience rather than theoretically. While facing my own major disappointment during that season, and in a state where I should have been crying and complaining about my disappointment, I was reminded that in everything I should give thanks. The word 'everything' simply means everything.

Observe that this is not a request, but a command God issues. There is never a situation in which we should stop giving thanks, no matter how bad.
Having learnt all these strategies does not mean we are immune to challenges. It means that when we do face them, we have a healthier approach to the setbacks. Having gone through my disappointment, and then receiving a call from one of my mentors who had been battling with a brain tumor for more than 4 years, and survived a near death attack the week prior to my compiling this lesson. Hearing her singing songs of thanksgiving to God and so tearful in gratitude for another chance to live, gave me a new perspective of my attitude and lack of gratitude in that season. I found myself thanking God for my disappointment even with tears in my eyes.

Saying thank you to God does not mean everything is in alignment and going according to plan, but it demonstrates your trust in God. Trusting Him according to His sincere promise that *"all things are working together for my good"*. That no matter how bad things are they will not always be like that because at some point God will answer you and the pain will end. I remember talking to a friend who had been in a relationship with an abusive spouse saying one of the most powerful statements I have heard.
She said *"I thank God for the pain I went through with this man. I thank God for the person I have become. This negative situation has given me the best gift of purpose."*

I found this to be so very profound, I don't think

during her tumultuous journey in abuse she felt this way. Obviously, it was hard, painful and heartbreaking that the person who was supposed to love her brought her so much untold misery. But had she gone through the painful years having seen the better future that was ahead, she would have gone through it with a better attitude.

Giving thanks helps to shift focus from negativity, because energy grows where energy goes, meaning that what you focus on grows bigger and bigger. Whatever you focus your mind on expands, that is why having a heart of gratitude opens room for you to receive more of the good things that God has in store for you. On the other hand, a person who does not have the attitude of gratitude can never be on speaking terms with happiness. This is because when you complain and grumble you create an atmosphere of anger and sadness which can also cripple your progress and growth. The Children of Israel are an example of this, who after seeing God's mighty hand of deliverance on their journey from Egypt still murmured and complained so much along the way. This resulted in an eleven-day journey becoming a forty-year journey such that most of the complainers did not arrive in the promised land.

You run the risk of not handling the things God promised you because of an ungrateful heart. Ungrateful people repel others because they are forever complaining, bitter and difficult to please.

Gratitude is the art of looking at life from a

different perspective. The ungrateful pessimist sees a glass to be half empty, while the grateful optimistic sees the glass to be half full. It is the same glass but two different perspectives. Always examine yourself and how you view things. It can tell you if you are a grateful person or not. One sure fact is that while you are in a state of complaining about your life, there is someone out there who is having it way worse than you, but they have learnt to be grateful.

Gratefulness is a condition of the heart that allows God to work greater things in your life. Like the story of the ten lepers who were healed by Jesus in Luke 17:11-19. After ten had received healing, only two came back to say "thank you" to Jesus. He went on to make them totally whole simply because of their heart of gratitude. When you express gratitude to God, you open room for greater miracles to happen to you, allowing more wins to come your way.

A thankful heart demonstrates a high level of faith that pleases God. The bible says in Romans 4:20-21 *"Abraham staggered not at the promise of God through unbelief, but was strong in faith giving glory to God."* This means that all the while as he waited for the fulfillment of his promise, he maintained a grateful heart against all odds. Before the manifestation of his son he was able to glorify God for making him a father of many nations even before his wife was pregnant. This kind of faith created things which were not there and eventually the promise was fulfilled.

Through the story of Lazarus, we also learn that thanksgiving has the ability to even bring to life those things we have lost. Jesus in his prayer just said, "I thank you father because you hear me always." And there after he instructed Lazarus to come forth and he rose up. It is thanksgiving that brought forth Lazarus from the dead. When you give thanks to God even in hopeless situations you unlock the potential for the miraculous. As you give thanks to God he intervenes in your situation and brings positive changes.

Thankfulness constantly reminds us that God is our source. If you know who your source is, you won't be angry at people or what they do, neither will you falter at the situations surrounding you because you have a Father who gives without fault-finding but gives liberally. Being grateful simply means sitting down and counting your blessings, it will surprise you what the Lord has done.
I've learnt the exercise of creating a daily ritual of finding at least ten things to thank God for before sleeping and as I wake up. This sends positive energy to my day, in my heart and around me and brings more blessings, peace and joy.

Exercise on Gratitude

Doing this exercise daily has brought so much joy to my heart and transformed the way I view hurts, trials and challenges. I have taken the portion of scripture that says "In everything give thanks" in its literal sense and I have started to incorporate it in my daily activities at another level. All I am doing is exactly what the verse is saying thanking God in every moment and situation whether it is good or bad. This also means that over and above counting my blessings, I am also acknowledging that I might not be where I want to be but because God already promised to grant the desires of our hearts, he will do it. I believe that God is in the process of sorting out those things that are causing me discomfort.

In practice It means that I am thanking God for those things I would otherwise complain about. For instance, I look at something in my life like my wardrobe and feel I really need more clothes. Instead of complaining about it what I would rather say is "Father I thank you for blessing me with clothes in my wardrobe, I thank you that no good thing will you withhold from them that walk up rightly and that you wish above all things that I may prosper, therefore I thank you that you are filling my wardrobe with beautiful clothes, abundance is my portion." Instead of complaining all I am doing is giving thanks in every area of my life, be it kids, husband, finances etc. I find a verse that highlights a promise in the area I have need and I thank him that he is already doing it.

With such an attitude I have no time to entertain anger and discouragement, because even in the painful situation I am seeing room for God to perform a miracle for me. It becomes joy all the way, no complaining or murmuring about things.

I encourage you to try it if it's something you haven't been doing already. Every moment you want to complain, visualize how you are likely to see God's intervention in that situation and thank him in advance for it. What a joy, peace and contentment this brings.

My daughter was fascinated when she would see me do this and even asked me why I talk when I'm alone. I explained to her that I am just filled with so much gratitude and I am thankful to God for the things he has done and is about to do. I have taught her to do this with me especially in the moments she comes to me complaining about something. Doing this continually has brought so much joy to me and made me emotionally content and whole. I shared this lesson with some ladies who were in a WhatsApp group I had been hosting and the following week some of them came with amazing testimonies of God's interventions as well as a sense of peace, joy and calmness in spite of the things they were facing during that time.

I realized that if someone could just get a quarter of what we have, they would be happy to have the things we are complaining about. Through this exercise I learnt that the things that God requires us to do don't necessarily benefit Him, but they are always for our good. When God asks us to give thanks, we do not change God or make him bigger because He is already an unchanging God. Even when you do not acknowledge it, it does not change him. As a matter of fact, we are the ones who benefit and change when we follow his instructions. It is our limited perceptions of God that change because when we give thanks in everything, we start seeing God in all his fullness and possibilities and our faith in him increases. This has the impact of shifting focus from our problems to God almighty who is our joy giver, way maker and promise keeper. When we see Him in that light, we are able to give him thanks always, eliminating all toxic and negative feelings that bring complaining and bitterness.

Another important thing is to teach our children to be grateful and thankful always. We need to be the first examples of what being grateful means and train them to be appreciative of all the blessings they have.

The truth is that it is a challenge when trouble comes our way, we can easily get clouded by events and grumbling sets in. As the children of Israel journeyed from Egypt to Canaan the land of promise, they would complain each time they would meet a hurdle and upset God. It took them forever to get to the promised land. My daily prayer is that the Holy Spirit would help me to have an attitude of gratitude always, to help me when I start complaining and bring me back in line with a grateful heart.

CHAPTER 12

CELEBRATING YOURSELF AND EVERY SMALL WIN

One of me most liberating lessons on my journey to emotional health was learning to celebrate myself - my small/micro wins as well as my big/macro wins. My background was one in which I grew up being celebrated so much for even the smallest achievements - by parents as well as family. This left me with an assumption that it is normal to be celebrated and thinking that all those around me would continue to celebrate me. My dad was a champion at celebrating each of us as children no manner how small our achievements. If you would hear him talking about us, his children he would go on and on about how proud he is of his children and parade our achievements at any opportunity he got. It can be a bit much at times and can get a little embarrassing how he can go on bragging about his children. As life has it, the realities of life always have a way of catching up with you when you leave that protective space your family offers. Getting out there into the world, in school, workplaces, marital relationships and the extended family that come with it brought new realities. One of my greatest shockers was that it was possible to actually go uncelebrated in certain spheres even after having done great things for those people you expect to celebrate you. For someone who grew up thinking it is normal to be celebrated, facing the realities of a world where your achievements can actually mean nothing to those you expect to celebrate you can lead to serious disappointment. If left unchecked, these experiences of not being celebrated can wilt your heart, kill your motivation to achieve greater things as well as break your morale. Going uncelebrated can create wounds and lead to feelings of disappointment due to unmet expectations.

Being celebrated motivates you to do greater things, boosts your moral and cultures a positive energy around you that propels you to a sense of wholeness. An interesting observation I have made is that the world celebrates what is already being celebrated and that what is celebrated is repeated. Most of the great accomplishments that come our way are a result of celebrated small wins. An example can be observed on a toddler, when they learn or achieve a new thing in their development such as a walking a few steps. Parents and people around the baby always get so excited about this milestone and celebrate it by saying "Yey! Good job! Well done! High five!" or whatever they do to show their baby that he/she is being celebrated. When celebrated, the child keeps repeating this act again and again and again. Why? Simply because they love the celebration and attention it brings.

This is just the same with us. We all have that heart of a child inside that longs to be celebrated when we do well. The truth is that energy goes where energy flows and when there is celebration it creates room for more celebration. The positive energy that comes with being celebrated will allow more wins to come your way. Celebration of your victories is manure and motivation for you to do greater things because what is celebrated is rewarded.

We all need and crave to be celebrated as it is one of our emotional needs. The challenge arises when you are not celebrated by those you expect to celebrate you. How we handle the disappointment and heartbreak of this unmet expectation to be celebrated is important for our overall wellness. The turning point for me was learning to love myself enough to celebrate myself and my achievements.

The first level is understanding that God almighty celebrates you and that he is very proud of you. Isaiah 62:4 explains this in a way I really love; *"Thou shalt no more be termed Forsaken; neither shall thy land any more be termed Desolate; but thou shalt be called Hephzibah and thy land Beulah; for the LORD delighteth in thee, and thy land shall be married."* Always remember that whatever it is you are doing, God is really proud of you, he is so much delighted in you and those things that you do well.

The Bible refers to God as a 'Rewarder,' He is always cheering you on and faithfully celebrates and rewards your achievements. Imagine what He did for Jesus at the time of his baptism, He literally showed up in the form of a dove and bragged in front of everyone present saying *"This is my beloved son in whom I am well pleased"* Matthew 3:17. That is how God really feels about us, He is well pleased in us. I have started turning to God more and more for his approval, and always remind myself that I am his beloved daughter and in me He is well pleased. God is so open and verbal about the way He celebrates us so when you have a need to be celebrated quickly turn yourself to God and remind yourself what he says about you.

The second thing is to just learn the art of celebrating yourself. Take time to introspect, considering your life, the things you have achieved and those you would like to achieve. For instance, you may want to gain an educational degree and you may not have a necessary subject like Mathematics to qualify for entry into the degree program. When you study the Math you didn't have and then succeed, make sure you celebrate this milestone. In as much as you have not begun the degree program, you are already making headway in achieving your big goal. Do not minimize this achievement or allow anyone else to minimize it, take a moment to celebrate it.

Always define what success means to you and make your own benchmark. Defining your success according to what others think means that when you fail to reach the benchmark set by others you will be disappointed and go uncelebrated for what you had viewed as success. Don't let other people rob you of your wow moments. You need to own and celebrate your journey and your story. Don't miss your moment to throw your own party when you have exceeded your own expectations. A joyful life is a life characterized by many mini celebrations that end up becoming a lifetime of celebration. You need not wait until you reach that big final goal for you to celebrate.

I came across a quotation somewhere that said *"Beware of destination addiction: the idea that happiness is in the next place, the next job, or even the next partner. Until you give up the idea that happiness is somewhere else, it will never be where you are"* (writer unknown). Don't reach the end of your life having lived a miserable, uncelebrated life simply because you ignored the small achievements waiting to celebrate only the big achievements.

A common belief is that it can be self-indulgent to celebrate yourself. This all depends on the state of the heart and the motive when you do it. The key is to do it from a place of pure self-love that appreciates and acknowledges that you are your best cheerleader and support. You can derive so much joy from celebrating yourself without being a brag.

Your question now may be how do I celebrate

myself? Here are some little things you can do in celebrating your achievements.

1. You can take daily reviews and acknowledge some of the things you feel you did well. For instance, you manage to go to the gym that day. Tell yourself that *"Samu I am proud that you made it to the gym today, well done and keep it up."* Words are power, and when you affirm yourself and verbally acknowledge your achievement you will be motivated to do it again tomorrow. It could be that you managed to get your driving learner's license. You may not be a driver yet, but this is an achievement towards the big goal. Celebrate it and reward yourself for it.

2. You need not break the bank to celebrate yourself. Simple gestures like getting yourself something as small as an ice cream or pampering yourself are ways of celebrating yourself. Other times it doesn't even have to cost you money, it can mean an extra hour sleeping, taking a walk, reading a book or doing something that makes you feel good. At times, I just enjoy listening to celebration music that really gets me going. You will be surprised what some music and a crazy dance can do for you as you celebrate yourself. When people celebrate, they dance to music because it has a very powerful and positive effect on you. A party isn't a good party when it is short of a good dance. Why not do your own celebration dance party in the kitchen for your achievement. You can even call your kids to this party and just release positive vibes that enable you to have a good time. I've

learnt that life is what you make it, a pity party is a choice, so is a celebration party.

3. Another thing you can do is share your achievement with people you know celebrate you. It could be your sister, your mum, or a close friend. Call them to celebrate with you. Make dinner, bake a small cake or whatever small thing that celebrates you. Celebrating your achievements is a way of showing your gratitude to God for enabling you. As you give thanks, you set a memorial and say "Ebenezer", thus far the Lord has brought me. You give God the glory for assisting you in achieving your goal.

Celebrating yourself brings you so much joy and heals your soul. It produces a positive energy that contributes to your overall wellness and emotional health. So my beloved friends what are you waiting for? It's time to get the party going celebrating you because you totally deserve it!

CHAPTER 13

LIVING A LIFE OF PURPOSE AND BECOMING A PERSON OF SIGNIFICANCE

While on this journey to emotional health it is necessary to establish why it is so important to become whole and emotionally healthy. One of my greatest realizations on my personal journey to wholeness was the extent to which brokenness distorted my understanding of my, true self and authentic identity. When one is confused about who they truly are this can limit the possibility of them fully living in true identity, divine calling and God given purpose. A state of complete wholeness is to be desired because brokenness can form barriers - mental and emotional limitations that can affect one's pursuit of their purpose.

"*Before I formed thee in the belly I knew thee, and before thou camest forth out of the womb I sanctified thee and ordained thee as a prophet unto the nations.*" Jeremiah 1: 5. God created each of us with a specific assignment and purpose which we need to fulfill. It is therefore important for each person to operate in their fullest capacity and whole state to be able to fulfill this purpose. God's intention is that you become someone of significance, whose journey on this earth will make an impact, and leave a footprint and legacy. Fulfilling your task on the earth can prove to be very difficult when you are carrying emotional wounds and other limiting challenges. A wounded soldier cannot fight in battle, this is also true about an emotionally wounded person, hence finding emotional healing is non-negotiable if one is going to be fully functional in fulfilling their assignment.

Satan is always lurking around to wound your soul because he is aware that your wholeness is a threat to his kingdom. His mission is clear - to steal, kill and destroy and he is working overdrive to ensure that you are that wounded soldier who is unable to fight in the battle. He knows that once you are whole and start living in your purpose, you become a threat to his kingdom. God on the other hand has seen the brokenness and pain in humanity and he is there to bring healing and wholeness.

Isaiah 61 talks about the process that leads to wholeness and the importance of becoming emotionally healthy.

Isaiah 61:1-4 (KJV) says, .
*The Spirit of the Lord God is upon me; because
the Lord hath anointed me to preach good tidings unto
the meek; he hath sent me to bind up the brokenhearted,*

*to proclaim liberty to the captives, and the opening of
the prison to them that are bound;*
*² To proclaim the acceptable year of the Lord, and the
day of vengeance of our God; to comfort all that mourn;*
*³ To appoint unto them that mourn in Zion, to give
unto them beauty for ashes, the oil of joy for mourning,
the garment of praise for the spirit of heaviness; that
they might be called trees of righteousness, the planting
of the Lord, that he might be glorified.*
*⁴ And they shall build the old wastes, they shall raise up
the former desolations, and they shall repair the waste
cities, the desolations of many generations.*

God is available and ready to bind up the brokenhearted and enable them to do great things in the earth such as building up the old wastes and repairing the desolate cities. You and I have responsibilities and tasks on this earth and the Lord needs us whole for these tasks and purposes He has called us for.

It is important to comprehend that your presence on this earth is not a cosmic accident, it was carefully planned for by the Almighty for a particular purpose you need to fulfill. God already predestined you for His purpose before you were made. When we began in the first chapter where I shared an exercise on exploring your authentic identity, part of the process was to help you take a closer look into your identity and unravel your interests as well as your purpose. I am aware that answering some of the questions in the exercise can be a grueling process and that you might still be investigating what your purpose is. It is important to rely on the Holy Spirit who is able to help you He will reveal it to you as you commit yourself to spend more time with Him.

My Journey to Purpose

I am so grateful that God revealed my purpose and I have chosen to take action as regards this purpose. I know that I am anointed to minister wholeness to others so that they can live out their God given purpose. Writing this book on the journey to emotional health is one action in fulfilling my divine purpose to minister wholeness to others. It is my prayer that people reading this book are ministered to and come to a place of wholeness and that those in need of emotional healing are being helped through this text. My desire is that people are able to become who God ordained them to become and that they are able to fulfill their purpose in spite of any emotional scars they carry from the past. The prayer made in 3 John 1:2, *"that I wish above all things that you may prosper and be in good health even as your soul prospers"* is also my prayer for those who come into contact with my ministry.

My journey to discovering my purpose began when I had just finished high school and was kind of in a fix not knowing what I was to do in life. At some point I had enrolled in some suspicious medical school which was just recruiting anyone who could afford it. I knew I was never meant to be a medical doctor but since I had no plan at that point I just jumped in for it. All in God's plan, this medical school turned out to be a fake one and closed after having chowed people's money. After this, my life didn't seem to have direction. Seeing people that I went with to school following their path and me stuck at home really depressed me. It was at that point I remember doing a 5 day, absolute fast, just to seek God's face about what he wanted me to do and become.

After this fast, the following Sunday God sent a lady to my church who was talking about women. Somehow deep in my heart I had a witness that my purpose in life was about women and I began looking for ways to pursue that. I approached one of my first mentors who was doing great things in this field Mrs Eunice Njovana who encouraged me to take action. The following year, miraculously I was in University studying about women. During this time, I began having serious unrest on issues of violence and abuse against women. It was during this period in 2004 while I was living at 102 Queensmead in Cape Town that I had a visitation of God in the story of Tamar. I knew in my heart that day that I was called to minister to those who are broken hearted and in a state of desolation. I knew that I was to help them from the place of pain and bring them to wholeness.

At that time, I didn't know how it was going to become a reality but I knew somehow it would come to pass. I began volunteering with Rape Crisis and trained in trauma, counselling of victims of rape. From that time even though I carried the vision in my heart, I only began working towards my vision and bringing it to reality 10 years later. I experienced a lot of pain, hurt and losses during the 10 years that caused me to forget who I really was (authentic identity). Now as I reflect on it with hindsight, it was necessary for me to go through that period of hardship and emotional trauma. Had I not gone through this phase, I realize now that I wouldn't be able to fully comprehend the pain and brokenness of people I counsel and minister to now. Indeed, there was purpose in my own painful journey. I only understood that later on in my journey.

Being able to make that journey back to me, from a place of brokenness to wholeness and finding my authentic identity has become a manual and road map that others can refer to on their own path to finding their wholeness. My journey enables me to speak and minister to others from an experiential place that is not only theoretical. These strategies I share with you are mostly based on my experiences, and lessons I learnt on my way to wholeness. I also find that it is easier for women to relate to them.

In 2014 I really felt it was time to take action with regards to my purpose and I went on to register the organization Tamar Restoration Centre. I still didn't know what to do or how to go about fulfilling this purpose. I prayed for God to show me what to do and give me direction and slowly began to take action from where I was. Until today I don't always know how to take the next step, but I continue to see God revealing where we are going layer by layer. Through this I learnt that you don't necessarily have to have it all figured out. What matters is to keep on moving because every step to fulfilling your purpose counts and provides material for God to work with. I have made a decision to live my purpose and minister wholeness to people from whatever platform available to me. That is my journey and I still await to see what lies ahead as God continues to direct me.

I share my experience to help someone think through the question of purpose. One thing is for sure - discovering your purpose will be a different journey for everyone, and everyone's purpose is unique and different. Some people are born knowing, like Samuel whose mum had already given him to God before he was born. Some will get God's visitation at a significant time in their lives like Mary mother of Jesus, Moses or Paul. Some have specific gifts that you can already identify like David who was a musician and Psalmist from a tender age. For some it's an unsettling feeling about things happening around you and you are always drawn to addressing it like the widow Dorcas in the Bible who had to be brought back to life because of how she was ministering to the poor. What is critical is that you discover that purpose and live it out.

Imagine the legendary Mother Theresa who touched so many lives in her special and unique way so much she couldn't be ignored. She left her footprint on the earth such that many years after she is gone, her life and work continue to speak to us. We all have the same challenge that when you do check out of this earth you should have emptied yourself, and left an indelible mark. We might not all have the biggest names but knowing in your life that you did what you were supposed to do and touched lives in the way you could- in your own unique way, is what really matters. The thing to be aware of is that your dream/ purpose is not about you. It's about the lives it will impact, so endeavor to live a life that continues beyond your life.

All you need to do is to find out that purpose and give yourself permission to work it.

Practical ways of living out your God given Purpose

1. Find Out What Your Purpose Is

It is important for you to be aware that there is a big reason why God allows you to continue to take in oxygen. Like I have mentioned, you are alive for a purpose. It is critical that you do not check out of this world having done nothing to

> *Significant people are ordinary people who choose to do extra ordinary things by living their purpose*

fulfill that God given purpose. The first most critical question you need to ask is "Why am I here?" This will automatically answer that nagging "Who am I?" question.

Ephesians 1: 18 *"I pray that the eyes of your heart may be enlightened in order that you may know the hope to which he has called you, the riches of his glorious inheritance in his holy people"*

God is the giver of purpose and He is also the revealer of purpose. You need to go to Him in prayer and ask Him to reveal your purpose. Many a times God shows up in the lives of people to clarify the purpose and he is always very clear. Abraham was told by God that he was to be the father of many nations. In Moses's case, God appeared to him at the burning bush encounter and sent him to become the great deliverer of the Israelites from the hand of Pharaoh. Joseph began having dreams from the time he was a youth and he knew he would do great things for his family and Israel. Jeremiah was visited by God at the age of 9 and God told him that he had ordained him prophet to the nations before his conception. The list of examples is endless in the Bible. God always showed up to the great men and women in the Bible to give them direction about their purpose. Know this thing for sure, God will reveal your purpose. Sometimes it's all a matter of timing but he will reveal. I had to fast for five days seeking God's face to receive direction for my life and the initial reveal. Thereafter it was a process of God directing me step by step. People's experiences will always be different, but what you need is to be connected to God for him to reveal.

One other thing that I have noted is that your purpose is linked to something that is a source of great joy for you. Do not ignore those moments when you have felt so much joy and fulfillment when doing something. They may be signs that your purpose is flowing in that direction. Sometimes you just have a hunch in you that this could be your purpose. Just follow its lead and ask God to reveal it. You might not get the full picture in one day, but what is critical is following God's lead and take action in the direction of your purpose.

2. Write it down Clearly

When you discover your purpose on the earth, it helps to write it down. Habakkuk 2: 2-3 says *"And the Lord answered me, and said, Write the vision, and make it plain upon tables, that he may run that readeth it. 3For the vision is yet for an appointed time, but at the end it shall speak, and not lie: though it tarry, wait for it; because it will surely come, it will not tarry."*

It is critical that you put your dream on paper. Write it very clearly in simple language you can understand, so that 'you can read even when you run.' This phrase means that a vision does not have to be complicated. When you put your thoughts on paper it is easier for you to articulate them. When you have written down the vision, it helps you come up with a road map for what you are going to do as well as the concrete actions that you are going to take to help you accomplish the vision. Writing it down clearly helps you to see where you are going.

Have tools that you treasure like a 'vision book' where you write those personal plans of where you see yourself in the future. A Vision Board is also a powerful tool which helps you visualize what you want the future to look like. There is power in visualization. That is what we saw Joseph do with his dreams. Eventually those dreams manifested and became reality. Having a clear vision helps you keep your eyes on the goal even when difficulties and challenges arise. The Bible even says, without a vision the people perish or cast-off restraint. Without a clear vision you leave your life to chance and things can easily go haywire. Give your vision time lines and goals that enable you to evaluate your progress. An example would be to say "by the end of the year I should be feeding five street kids". That is a goal with a time-line for a vision to minister to street kids.

3. Find Mentorship
As you walk on your journey to finding your purpose, it is important that you find mentors who can hold your hand on this journey. The Bible says that "*In the multitude of counselors there is life*" Proverbs 11:14. Pray that God gives you like minded dream builders, who are faithful enough to incubate your dream and give you all the support you need. I was so blessed that God has been faithful to surround me with the wisest and supportive destiny helpers. Mrs D Mukwena and Mrs E Njovana are my first mentors who continue

to stand with me until today. I have been so blessed to have the likes of Pastor Cynthia Chirinda. When I met her, I just had the vision and didn't know what to do. She just started planning the first workshop with me and has been present all the way to give wisdom and guidance. I also have Pastor Rumbidzayi Kamba who has been so instrumental in growing my faith and linking me to great people until I received an award for the work I had been doing.

All I am saying is, you need Mentorship in your journey. Find people who have travelled a similar trail to the one you would like to travel and learn as much as you can from them. Sometimes you might not know what to do with regards to working your purpose and all you need is just another perspective to help you see what you are not seeing.

4. Take action

For any vision to take off, you need to take action and do something about your purpose. Always be aware that our time here on earth is limited, so don't waste your days, weeks, months and years without doing anything in line with your vision. Indeed, there is an appointed time for the vision to blossom, but it takes small actions to bring the big picture together. Put your vision into bite size goals and work these small goals. A journey of a thousand miles begins with one step. At times the vision looks so big and insurmountable. Imagine that your vision is to build a school. You don't shove the vision away because you don't have anything to begin with, just start right where you are. This might mean tutoring one student at a time and then converting your garage into classrooms. You will be amazed how far the universe will start creating more room for you.

Don't let money or resources stop you from taking small actions that will help you fulfill vision. I remember when I started to do community outreaches with TRC. I would work with a budget of 20$ZW bond, this included the snacks I would prepare from my home, sandwiches, cupcakes, and Mazoe cordial juice as well as bus fare for me and my team. When a person sees pictures of those events you would think a donor poured in money, but it was just small money I raised from my peanut butter and cake business which I used to finance my vision.

To make an impact you don't necessarily need to rent offices. All you need is to be innovative. When I began my online work on the journey to emotional health all I needed was to open a WhatsApp group and Facebook page and begin to minister wholeness to others and live out my purpose. It did not require any capital or cost me anything more than other people using these same platforms for free. All I am saying is eliminate excuses and start working your vision. Take action because when many small actions are added together they look big. Don't despise whatever action you need to take, no matter how small. Take action and keep on moving. Remember to celebrate those small victories along the journey to the fulfilment of your vision.

5. Keep taking Action

Your purpose is for life, do not stop. Keep taking action. Review what you have done in the past, and improve on it. Don't be afraid to make mistakes, because that is how you learn and grow. Give yourself many second chances, and press reset if you must.

Don't be intimidated by what others are doing. Run your own race. We are all unique, so do you. Be unapologetically you! Be original, and don't try to be a carbon copy of anyone else. Why don't you be the best version of you instead of a lousy imitation of someone else. There is a reason God put that DNA in you, that laughter, that crooked tooth like mine. All this makes me relevant and enough for the job God has tasked me. So my friends, work your dream and empty yourself so that when you stand before the Father one day he will say 'well done!'. Seek to impress God, you will always find people who are not impressed by you.

CONCLUSION

It is my hope that going through this journey has opened your eyes to a new realm of wholeness. Being Emotionally Healthy can be described as a state of being in control of one's thoughts, feelings and behaviors. It simply means being aware of one's emotions and how to deal with them whether negative or positive. Being emotionally healthy does not mean that you don't feel anger, frustration, stress or sadness, but the focus is on how one deals with all these emotions in a healthy way. Emotional Health can lead to success as happy people are more likely to work towards their goals and find resources they need as well as attract others with their energy and optimism. Being emotionally healthy also equips one to build resilience that enables them to bounce back when they are faced with curve balls and tough times in their lives.

The state of being emotionally unhealthy has the capacity to paralyze the soul, resulting in a loss of focus and will power to go on. As a result of this realization, I became more compassionate towards people even those who commit suicide (although I still do not condone it); simply because we have no idea what people go through that overwhelms them to the extent of feeling they have no other choice but to die.

The place of desolation is a clear-cut fulfillment of the devil's mission in John 10:10, "to steal, to kill and to destroy". We are grateful that Jesus came endowed with power to counter this mission. He says that He came to give us life in abundance. Instead of the state of desolation one might find themselves in, there is an offer for you to receive abundant life that comes from Christ Jesus. 3 John 2 puts it this way, "*Beloved, I wish above all things that thou mayest prosper and be in health, even as thy soul prospereth*" God's desire for us is to be well and whole in spirit, soul and body. In as much as God provides healing for your body, he likewise provides healing for your soul. Emotional Health is a tool which can bring desired health to your ailing soul and give you tools to succeed when you go through turbulent times emotionally. We live in a fallen world with imperfect people, as such, time and again things that will hurt us and challenge the health of our souls will be thrown at us and bring us to that desolate place. It is important that we pursue our wholeness so that we live the peaceable, joyful and abundant life that Christ offers. It is therefore your responsibility to pursue your wholeness because the bulk of the times those that hurt you are not coming to fix you. Your healing is your responsibility and flipping the pages of this book is one way in which you are actively pursuing your wholeness

Hoping to meet you all on the grandstand of 'Significant People'. We are Victors and never victims of our circumstances

THE END

ABOUT THE AUTHOR

Drawn to the plight of women, Samukile Takavingofa has dedicated her life to building resilience and capacity in women to overcome life's challenges and curve balls. Following her divine encounter while she was still in college, she knew after that day that she was called to lift women from desolation and anointed to minister wholeness. Samu is the Founder of Tamar Restoration Centre (TRC), an Emotional Health Life Coach, Gender Specialist, Transformational Speaker and counselor. She believes that women's mental and emotional wholeness is key to flourishing lives as well as fulfilling their God given purposes. Driven by her passion to minister wholeness she facilitates a Christian Life-skills programme called "The Journey to Emotional Health" which has benefited many women. She has also recently begun hosting a groundbreaking online talk show titled "Stories of Hope from Brokenness to Wholeness". Her work was recognized at the Pan African Humanitarian Summit awards where she was awarded for Gender Advocacy and Empowerment. Samukile is wife and mother of three beautiful children

To book your session and connect to the author:
Facebook Page: Journey to Emotional Health with Samu
E-mail: samutakavingofa@gmail.com
Tel: +1 202 820 7801